THE ZEN CHARACTER:
LIFE, ART AND TEACHINGS OF ZEN MASTER SHINZAN MIYAMAE

THE ZEN CHARACTER: LIFE, ART AND TEACHINGS OF ZEN MASTER SHINZAN MIYAMAE

Edited by Julian Daizan Skinner

Contributors:
John Stevens PhD
Audrey Yoshiku Seo PhD
Julian Daizan Skinner
Members of the Zenways Sangha

Copyright © 2015 by:
Julian Daizan Skinner All rights reserved.

First paperback edition printed 2015 in the United Kingdom

ISBN 978-0-9931981-1-3

No part of this book shall be reproduced or transmitted in any form or by any means, electronic or mechanical, including photocopying, recording, or by any information retrieval system without written permission of the publisher.

Published by Zenways Press. Printed and bound by Ashford Colour Press Ltd, Gosport, Hants PO13 0FW

ACKNOWLEDGEMENTS

This volume is produced on the occasion of the eightieth birthday of Zen master Shinzan Miyamae. In celebrating his life, artworks and teachings, we are particularly grateful to the following contributors:

Photos from:
Gerry McCulloch (senior lecturer at Goldsmiths College, University of London),
Hogetsu Bärndal,
Alex Horikitsune Reinke,
Mark Westmoquette PhD,
Audrey Yoshiku Seo PhD,
Melody Eshin Cornell.

Written contributions from:
Audrey Yoshiku Seo PhD,
Professor John Stevens (University of Sendai, retired),
Julian Daizan Skinner,
Members of the Zenways sangha.

Editor:
Julian Daizan Skinner

Design:
Monika Müller

Cover Design:
Tony Green (Ideology)

Design Editor:
Mark Westmoquette

Transcription/editing:
Dainei Tracy

Proofreaders:
Samantha Warrington
David Bernstein
Mark Westmoquette PhD

With grateful thanks to:
Matt Shinkai Kane
Alex Horikitsune Reinke
Horiyoshi III Nakano Yoshihito
Barbara Ryusen Gabrys
Matt Gregory

CONTENTS

INTRODUCTION 13

OUTSIDE THE BOX: MAVERICK ZEN MASTERS 19

CATALOGUE OF CALLIGRAPHIES BY SHINZAN RŌSHI 35

APPRECIATING ZEN ART: AN INTERVIEW WITH AUDREY YOSHIKO SEO, ZEN SCHOLAR 127

ZEN MASTER SHINZAN – A LIFE IN FIVE CALLIGRAPHIES 133

TALKS ON PRACTICE BY ZEN MASTER SHINZAN 165

ENCOUNTERS WITH SHINZAN RŌSHI 181

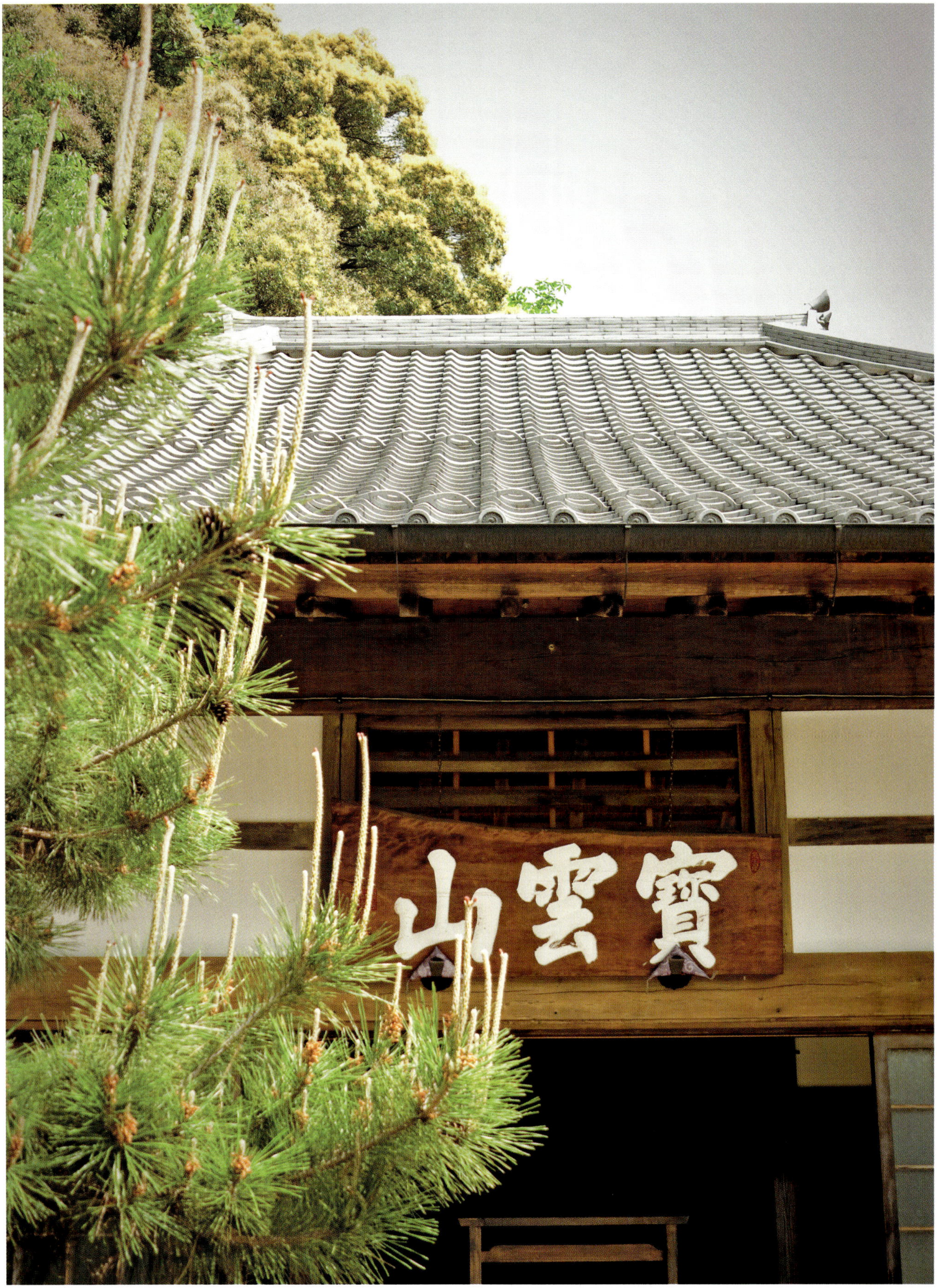
寶雲山

© 大法
月 BAERNDAL

INTRODUCTION

by Julian Daizan Skinner

One day in the knee-to-knee encounter of sanzen (the Zen interview between teacher and student), Master Itsugai looked intensely at Shinzan, his student, pointed to his own eye and said, "As surely as my pupil is black, you are worthy to be the Zen master of Shōgenji."

This affirmation followed many years of Shinzan's Zen practice. Many more were to follow, at Shōgenji and elsewhere.

In the Zen tradition, the archetype for this type of encounter concerns the Buddha: "Once, in front of his gathered assembly on Vulture Peak, the Buddha silently held up a flower. There was no response save for his senior student, Makakashyo, who smiled. The Buddha announced, "I possess the eye and treasury of the truth. I bestow it on Makakashyo".

This founding story of Zen transmission has been treasured and passed down through the generations to the present day. The holding up of a flower and the smile are seen as manifestations of spiritual equality—the new ancestor is a worthy successor of the previous one. Simultaneously, there is a recognition of hierarchy—the previous ancestor affirms the new one.

In many fields of human activity involving an educational process or apprenticeship, there naturally comes a moment where the teacher perceives that the student is ripe. Scholars typically deny the historicity of the Vulture Peak incident and that psychological truth and historical truth are mismatched. Nevertheless, the effect of this framework has coloured centuries of Zen practice down to the present day. One definition of Zen holds that this transmission, this equal and yet unequal meeting, is its true nature.

Arising out of this foundation story is the concept of lineage—masters naming successors down through history. Within India, it is possible to find lineages amongst the esoteric or Vajryana versions of Buddhism (although not stretching back to the historical Buddha); not so in the case of Zen. Nevertheless we can find suggestive concepts. The Buddha spoke of a student who had awakened as having achieved *gotra-bu nana*—literally "change of family" or "change of lineage" insight. Now the student has joined the family or lineage of the noble ones. This change of lineage happens, however, whether or not it is recognised by anyone.

Within Zen, particularly as it developed in China and Japan, the sense of the teacher being an arbiter was greatly heightened. Here we find in full form the two aspects mentioned above—the student's enlightenment and the teacher's affirmation. Deviations also arose. Sometimes elaborate ceremonial forms enshrined this simple human encounter. Sometimes the form was re-interpreted to take on the quality of an initiation. Perhaps the most extreme derivation of Zen's foundation story denies the necessity of the enlightenment of either the teacher or the student. The transmission is considered passed-on as long as the correct ritual procedures are followed.

In many cases, physical artefacts symbolising this transmission were handed on by the teacher. Systems of certification were also widespread. Some of the most eminent teachers, including the famous 18th century Zen master Hakuin, received neither.

In the case of Shinzan, his master, Itsugai Rōshi, wanted him to receive the transmission paperwork from a senior student. Concerned that this man's spiritual eye was not yet opened (Itsugai Rōshi concurred), Shinzan believed that this process could only dilute what had already transpired and opted not to receive it. Nevertheless, as he said to me, "They all called me 'Rōshi', 'Rōshi'."

After a long study period at Shōgenji (at the time nicknamed the "devil's dōjō" for the strictness of the training) as well as other Zen monasteries, Shinzan restored the abandoned hermitage of the great 17th century Tokugawa Zen master, Bankei Yotaku. His intention was to restore the Zen school's emphasis on enlightenment. He put up a sign at the gate, "Place for young and old people to experience satori," (literally "awakening") and focused his work on helping each entrant become, what he calls "a true person."

There is in Zen the conception of lifelong development. Shinzan Rōshi has often remarked to me how practice in his seventies is so much deeper than it was in his sixties. Japanese culture is influenced by Confucius' teaching: "At fifteen my heart was set on learning; at thirty I stood firm; at forty I had no more doubts; at fifty I knew the will of heaven; at sixty my ear was obedient; at seventy I could follow my heart's desire without overstepping the boundaries of righteousness." The potter, the artist, the student of life, all are seen as growing in this way. If it is true, this development benefits others as well as oneself. In the 14th century English manual of contemplation, 'The Cloud of Unknowing', we find:

> "Whoever has this work, it should govern him very graciously, in body as well as in soul, and make him very favourable to each man or woman who looks upon him; to the extent that the least favoured man or woman that lives in this life, if they can, by grace, come to labour in this work, their features would be changed suddenly and graciously, so that each good man who saw them would be glad and joyful to be in their company".

To meet someone genuinely "in this work" is a privilege and a blessing. Year by year this blessing grows. Within the culture of East Asia, mastery of the brush encompasses the highest of all artforms. There is a long-standing tradition (as there is also in the West) that the character is communicated directly through the writing. For centuries, collectors have gathered samples of the writing of admirable people.

There are many styles of calligraphy. The Zen style, called in Japanese, bokuseki, "ink traces", is often characterised by bold, assertive and informal brush strokes embodying the calligrapher's enlightened presence. Technique, clarity and comprehensibility are all considered less important than this directness. A Westerner, who doesn't read characters and an Easterner who does, may not be in a very different position when it comes to "reading" the work of the Zen masters. Bokuseki invites a heart-level meeting with the artist's presence transmitted through the encounter of brush and paper. For those of us unable to live day-to-day with a Zen master, the "glad and joyful" presence spoken of by The Cloud of Unknowing above can thus be touched through living with the artwork.

This can be found, for example, in the apogee of Japanese culture, the tea ceremony. Although, architecture, garden design, flower-arranging, cuisine, ceramics and many other arts contribute, they can all be seen as providing the perfect context in which to encounter the awakened awareness within the centrepiece—the scroll painted by a Zen master hanging in the teahouse alcove.

Generally speaking, Zen masters will turn their attention towards painting and calligraphy in later years. The works here are created after half a century of full-time Zen cultivation by a fiercely independent master. It is my hope that this little book will give you sufficient background and translation to facilitate your direct acquaintance with the Zen character presented by Shinzan Rōshi. May this immediate encounter serve to ignite the torch of understanding within you so that you too may become a true person.

Juran Daizan
February full moon 2015
Yugagyo Dōjō
Camberwell
London

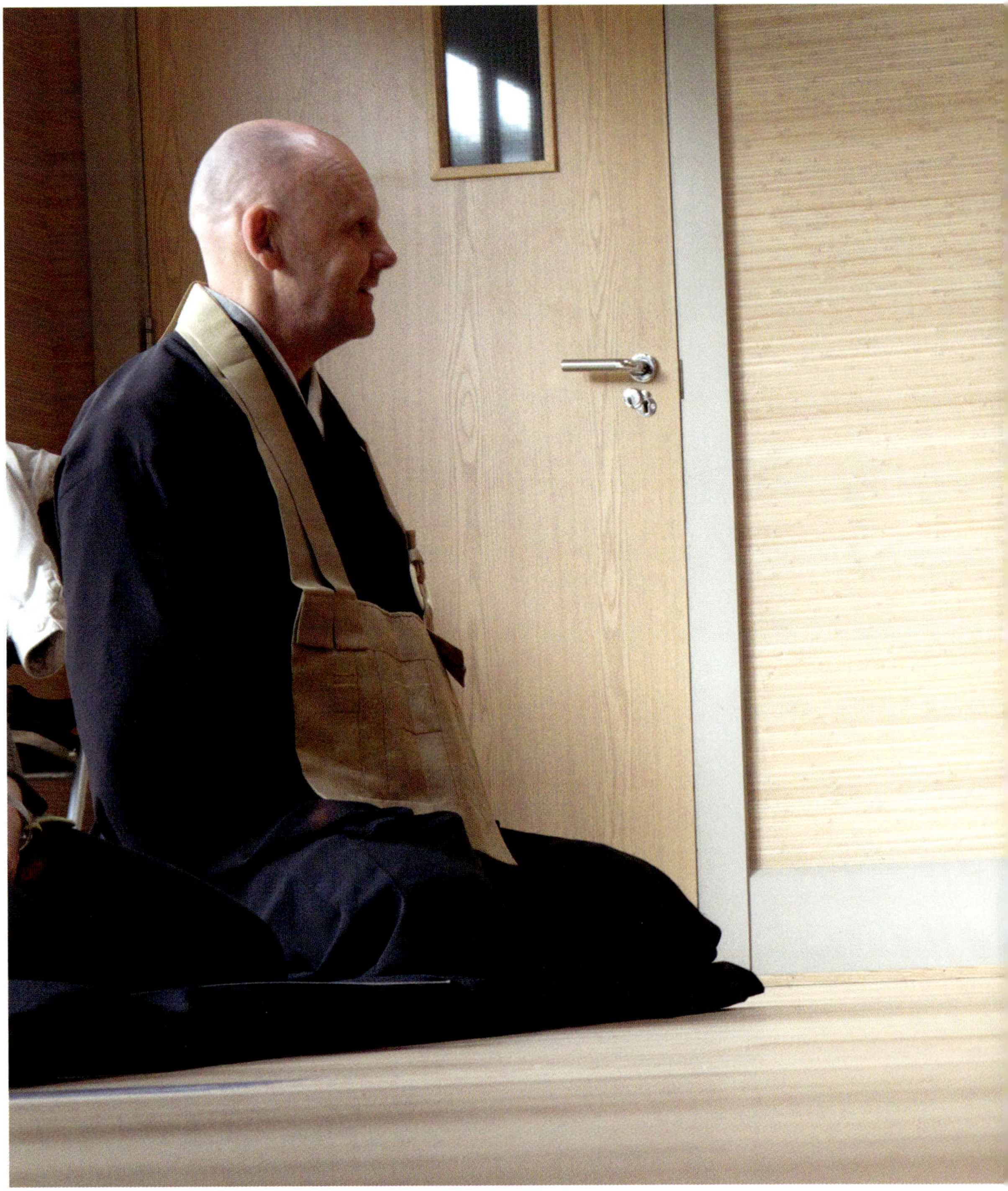

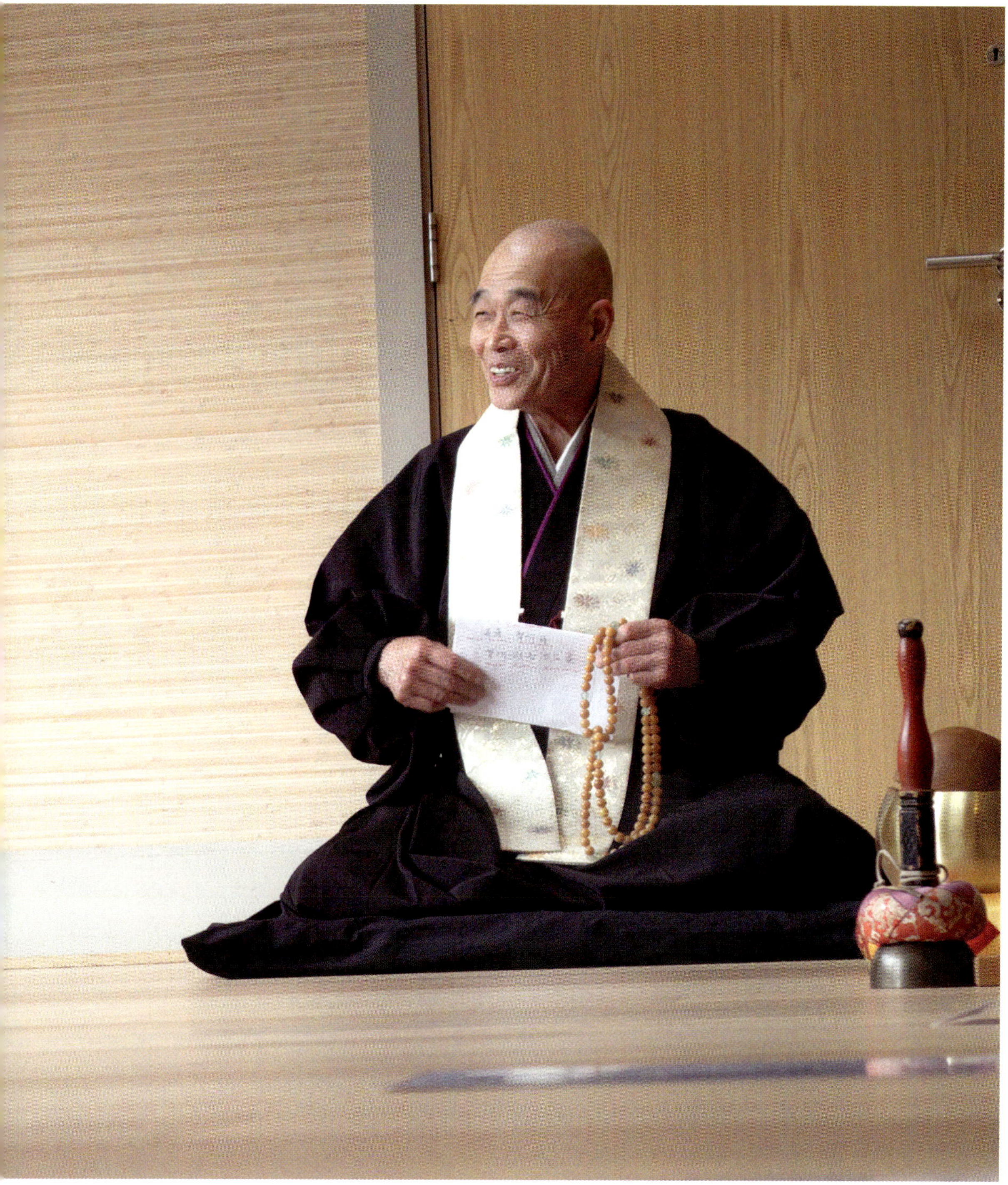

OUTSIDE THE BOX: MAVERICK ZEN MASTERS

by Audrey Yoshiko Seo

Zen is known as a religion of contradiction, a religion that does not rely on words, yet which abounds in rich texts. It is a long tradition based on transmission from master to student, all striving to uphold and maintain adherence to the practices of masters before them. Yet, within this pure tradition and strict practice, there have been those Zen masters through the ages who have approached their teachings in somewhat unconventional ways. These masters, all of whom strove to preserve the past, also acknowledged the necessity to understand their present; foster the past by being in the moment. Shinzan Miyamae Rōshi is a current example of a Zen master who, despite his strict traditional training, has made choices as a teacher and spiritual leader to understand current social situations. While this has brought both criticism and praise, it also reveals Zen's ability to adapt, evolve and constantly consider its ever-changing audience. This history of Zen masters who occasionally "step outside the box" includes some of the most prominent and influential figures, including Ikkyū, Hakuin, Ryōkan, and Nantenbō.

Ikkyū (1394-1481)

Perhaps the most notorious of the "renegade" Zen monks was Ikkyū, who lived largely outside the confines of the monastic institution and, in fact, was hardly a monk in the traditional sense at all since he observed so few of the regulations that set a monk apart from society. Yet by stripping himself of the outward affectations of Zen practice, he was able to bare witness to its fundamental core, helping to solidify a true sense of Zen during the Muromachi period (1392-1573), and enabling Zen to be absorbed more deeply and profoundly into Japanese culture. After studying for three years with the eccentric master Ken'o (?-1414), and seven years under the strict master Kasō (1352-1428), a monk of the Daitoku-ji line, Ikkyū had his first breakthrough, and two years later attained full enlightenment on a summer's evening upon hearing the cry of a crow. Ikkyū had already developed a sense that temples and monasteries were too removed from the active world of everyday people and, as a result, he believed many monks had lost their Buddha-nature becoming overly concerned with institutionalised rituals and routines.

Ikkyū's strict view of Zen developed into an opposition to anything that he saw as the bastardisation of Zen, as well as a dislike for the "aristocratic Zen" that catered only to the seats of power for the sake of wealth and advancement. Instead, Ikkyū sympathised with the common people, and was drawn to expressing Zen in ways understandable to a broader audience. To this end, he is credited with being the first to popularise kana hōgo, the writing of Zen sermons in colloquial Japanese, making them much more approachable.

Ikkyū did not consider this a dilution of Zen teaching, but simply a transmutation into a more effective medium.

Beyond his efforts to spread Zen teachings to the masses, Ikkyū was also highly critical of monks and priests whose interests seem to lie largely in the financial benefits of temples, particularly Daitoku-ji, and accused them of "selling Zen" by easing up on Zen practice in order to make the temple more profitable. When Kyoto was ravaged by a series of natural disasters in the mid-15th century including drought, crop failure, and plague, followed by the Ōnin Wars in 1467, Ikkyū despaired at the human tragedy and fled to Sumiyoshi in 1469. In Sumiyoshi he met a 40-year-old blind singer named Mori, who became the love of his later life and the subject of over a dozen poems. It is this aspect of physical love and sexuality that sets Ikkyū apart from not only his contemporaries, but all Zen masters of the past. Ikkyū wanted his Zen to be raw, direct and authentic, this included being totally upfront about sex: "When thirsty, one dreams of water; when cold, one dreams of a warm robe. My nature is to dream of the pleasures of the bedchamber!" For Ikkyū, sexual desire was just something that became a part of his life and he dealt with it as part of his everyday existence.

Ikkyū arguably possessed the most dynamic calligraphic hand of the period, and became increasingly involved in the arts, writing inscriptions on paintings brought to him and doing his own works of calligraphy and a few paintings of his own. His great sense of conviction and strength of character stands out in his calligraphy which is known for its vitality. A wooden board carved from Ikkyū's brushwork reads, "Silent Seeing" (Fig. 1). Here we see Ikkyū's unique combination of elegance and energy in the brushstrokes that tilt and dance, reflecting Ikkyū's own restlessness and sense of urgency.

Even a maverick such as Ikkyū had to temper his convictions and consider the benefits of the whole; during the Ōnin War, he was asked to serve as abbot of Daitoku-ji, now reduced to ashes by the war. With the temple's very continuance in question, Ikkyū could not refuse, even if it meant returning to institutionalised Zen. His sense of personal conflict and even shame are revealed in a poem he wrote marking his return and referring to the purple robed bestowed upon him by the emperor as a mark of high rank,

> Daitō's descendants destroyed his remaining light
> Hard to melt the heart in song on an icy night
> For 50 years, a wanderer with straw raincoat and hat,
> Shameful today, a purple-robed monk.[1]

After the war, Ikkyū dutifully and energetically began collecting contributions to rebuild Daitoku-ji, and while donations were generous from feudal families who had long supported Daitoku-ji, ironically contributions also emerged from the broad range of ordinary people with whom Ikkyū had spent years associating. Thus, after struggling with the establishment in the name of preserving the spiritual integrity of Daitoku-ji for so long, Ikkyū's ultimate achievement was the re-establishment of the monastery's material existence as well.

Fig 1: Ikkyū Board "Silent Seeing", Carved Wood, 24 x 68 cm., Private Collection (reproduced with permission from Dr. Seo)

---

1 Sonja Arntzen, Ikkyū and the Crazy Cloud Anthology: A Zen Poet of Medieval Times (Tokyo: University of Tokyo Press, 1986), p.31.

© 木法
月 BAERND

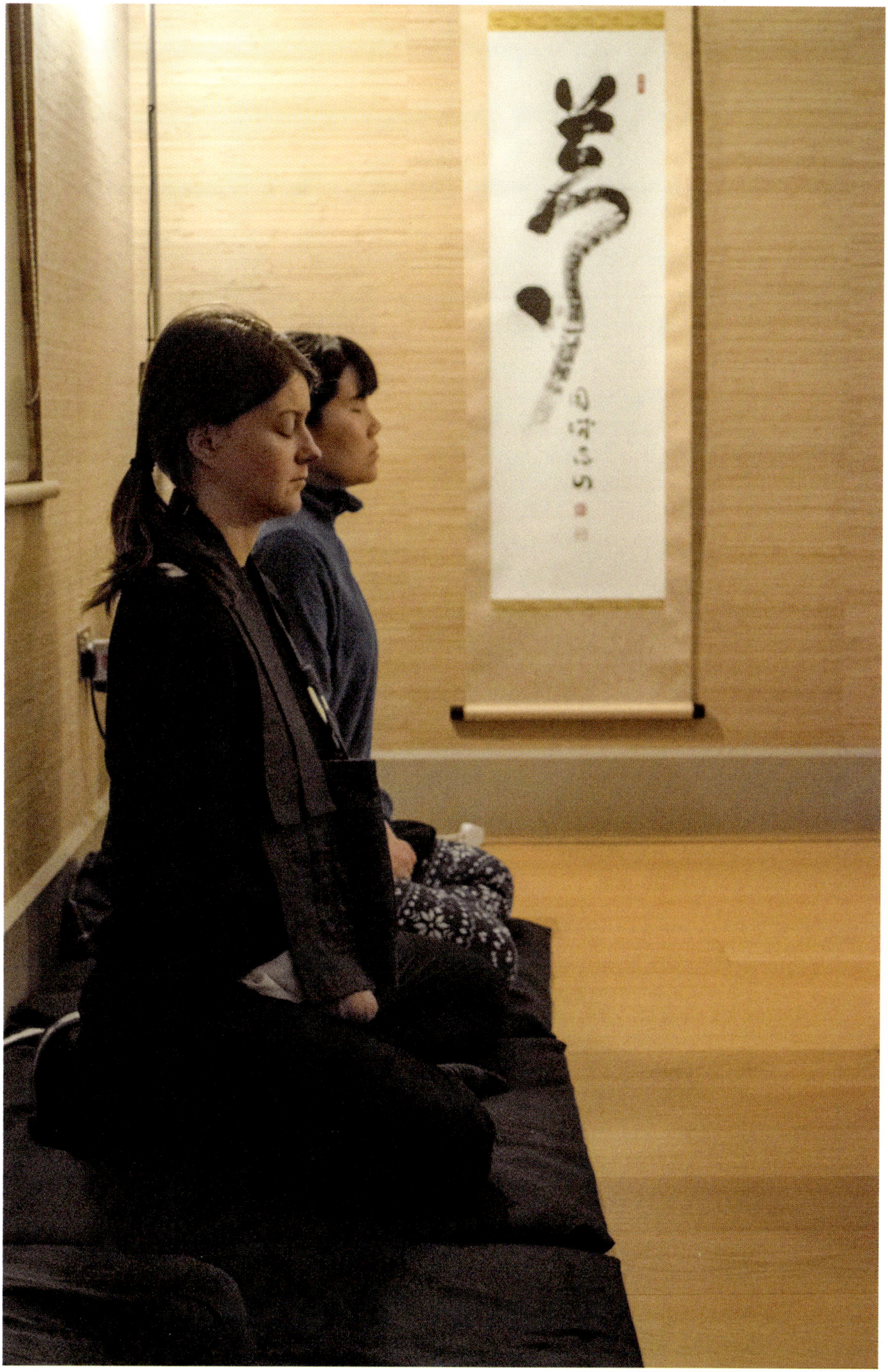

In the last six years of his life, Ikkyū oversaw the restoration of all the major buildings of Daitoku-ji and three of its sub-temples. He died in the winter of 1481, passing away while seated in meditation. Ikkyū vehemently disagreed with the institutionalised aspects of Daitoku-ji. He lived a different life from the conventions of monastic bureaucracy, and strove to bring Zen to a wider audience—to bring the ideals of the wondrously ordinary to which Zen aspires to everyday people. Thus, despite his heretical beliefs and unconventional practices, Ikkyū is considered one of the greatest Zen masters of the Daitoku-ji lineage.

Hakuin Ekaku (1685-1768)

Known as the "revitaliser of Rinzai Zen in Japan" despite spending most of his career in a small rural temple, Hakuin achieved this accolade by restructuring Zen training methods, by deepening monastic practice, by insisting upon "post-enlightenment" training, and by consciously and enthusiastically reaching out to lay parishioners in new ways. As a result of his reorganisation of Zen monastic training, as well as his sheer force as a teacher and Zen lecturer, Hakuin's position in Zen history was solidified. In fact, today virtually all Japanese Rinzai Zen monks and priests can trace their training lineages back to Hakuin through one of his dharma grandsons, Inzan Ien (1751-1814) or Takujū Kosen (1760-1833). In all, the revitalised form of Zen that Hakuin left was significantly and sufficiently rejuvenated enough that it became widely acknowledged as "Hakuin Zen" and was passed down through his numerous disciples, revamping Zen monastic training as it entered the modern age.

Hakuin had begun accepting a few students in his late thirties and early forties. However, by the early 1740s when he was in his fifties, people from all stations of society and representing all occupations came flocking from throughout Japan as word of his Zen teachings spread across the country. Although a fierce teacher with his Zen disciples, Hakuin had great respect, sympathy and warmth for his lay followers. Just as he was determined to lead his monastic disciples down the true path of *kenshō* (self-realisation), he also hoped to lead the general populous to the Buddhist truth. At the same time, he was keenly aware of different lifestyles and thus, different limitations and obstacles. As a result of this broader and more varied audience, Hakuin developed new ways of modifying or adapting his teaching methods. Aware that many of his lay followers had little or no education and had lived completely different life experiences, Hakuin approached them accordingly. Building on Ikkyū's use of *kana hōgo*, he incorporated folk and popular themes and images into his paintings, writings and sermons in order to convey his Zen teachings through more familiar and identifiable contexts.

Fig 2: Hakuin, Portrait of Daruma, Ink on Paper, 126 x 55 cm., Chikusei Collection (reproduced with permission from Dr. Seo)

Beyond the huge number of important Zen manuscripts that Hakuin left, he is widely known for the abundance of paintings and calligraphies he created, most of which were given to monastic disciples and lay followers as gestures of encouragement and reminders of the Zen truth. Hakuin may have believed that certain subjects were particularly suited as Zen examples for particular followers, while other works were probably given to monks from other temples who admired Hakuin's Zen teachings. Hakuin was particularly noted for his images of Daruma (Bodhidharma), the First Patriarch of Zen (Fig. 2), the most traditional and common subject among Zen paintings. On this image, painted late in Hakuin's life, he has inscribed, "See Your Own Nature and Become Buddha," a phrase attributed to Daruma. However, at the same time, Hakuin developed dozens of new subjects, most of which probably originated from his own personal experiences and daily encounters. During the Edo period, the Korean government sent regular diplomatic delegations including musicians, dancers, and other performers to Japan, and Hakuin was probably familiar with these events. Hakuin captured the marvels of Korean trick horseback riders (Fig. 3) performing in brightly colored tunics as they emerge from a large gourd in the lower right corner. This is possibly a reference to the Zen idea that even the most remarkable things can come from the seemingly ordinary.[2] In the lower left Hakuin has written,

Koreans with their foreign saddles—
Galloping, galloping in unison.
Bending, twisting, jumping on and off.
Jumping on and off.

Aside from his art, Hakuin also composed simple songs to use as forms of teachings, again utilising colloquial speech to convey complex Zen themes to ordinary people. His most famous of these popular songs is the "*Zazen Wasan*" (Song of Meditation) in which he praises meditation in a clear, straightforward manner. Hakuin believed that not only should meditation and Zen practice permeate daily life, but that daily life must permeate practice. Spiritual leaders, like government officials, were largely useless if they could not assist others in the world at large. For Hakuin, Zen was a means to *kenshō* for all beings in all situations and stations of life. Just as each individual brought his or her own experiences to Zen practice, the Zen experience must be taken back into the world in order to flourish and fully aid people in their journey.

Fig.3: Hakuin, "Korean Acrobats", Ink and Colour on Paper, 44.5 x 56.5 cm., Behr Collection (reproduced with permission from Dr. Seo)

2 There is a Japanese phrase, "*Hyôtan kara, koma ga deru,"* ("Horses emerge from the gourd").

木法
月 BAERNDAL

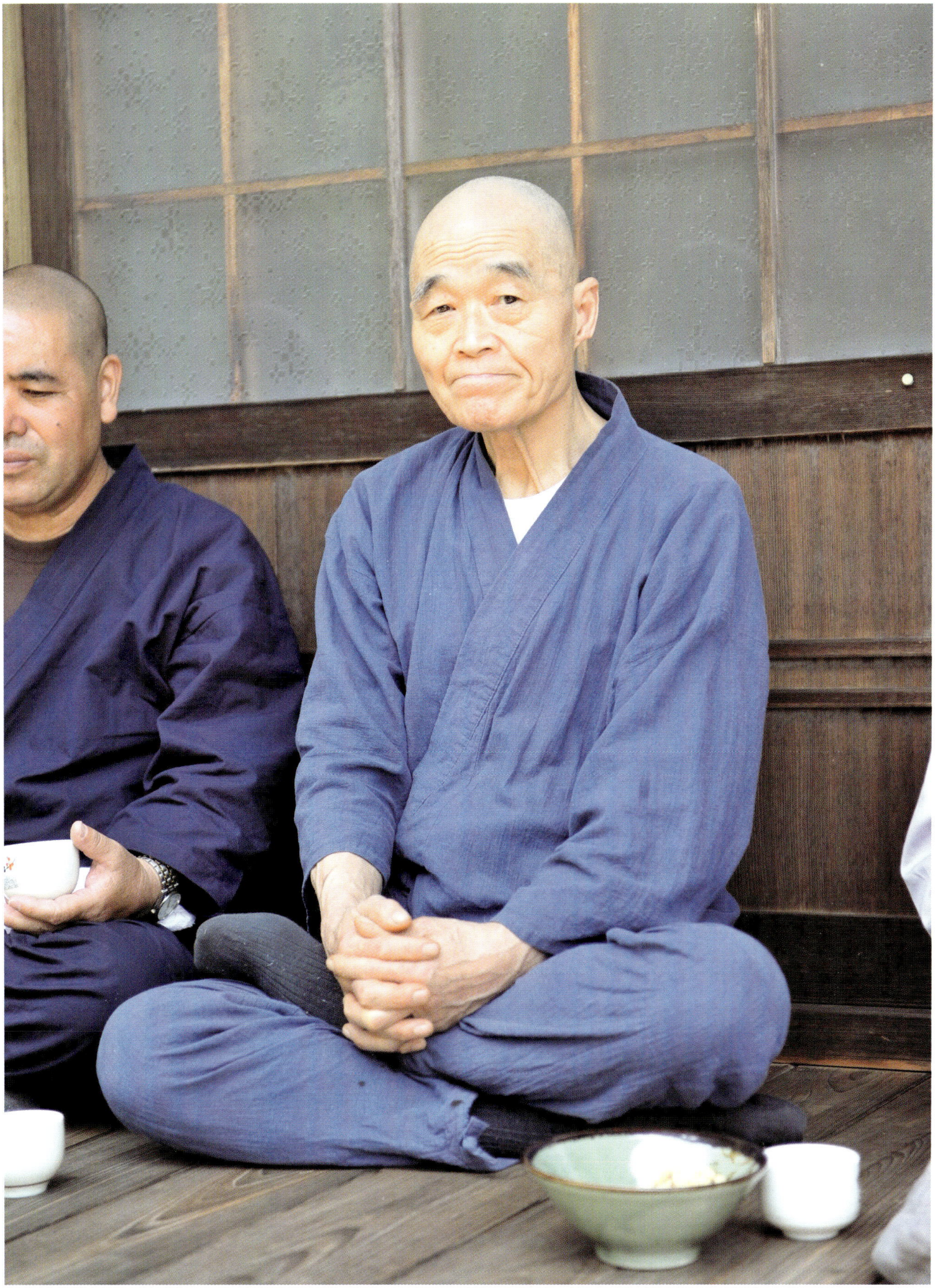

Ryōkan (1758-1831)

While Ikkyū lived largely outside the monastic system until he was called upon to return to Daitoku-ji in his later years, and Hakuin worked tirelessly within the monastic system from a small rural temple, the eccentric poet Ryōkan represented a different type of Zen figure. Ryōkan studied under the Sōtō master Kokusen, abbot of Entsū-ji, for more than ten years until his master's death in 1791, receiving Kokusen's dharma transmission in the process. Unhappy with temple life after Kokusen's death, Ryōkan left Entsū-ji and set out as a wandering monk. Ryōkan's mother had died in 1783, and in 1792 his father committed suicide in Kyoto for unknown reasons. Ryōkan attended memorial services for his father and remained in the Kyoto area for the next year or so. Then, in 1796, he abruptly returned to his native Izumozaki, Echigo Province (Niigata), where he lived out the rest of his life, living at various temples and lodgings until 1804, when he moved into the Gogō-an, a small hut near Kokujō-ji temple. Ryōkan lived at the Gogō-an for 13 years, but eventually his advanced age deemed it necessary for him to move to more accessible lodgings. He died in 1831 at the age of 73 after living in a renovated storehouse owned by a friend in Shimazaki. Although Ryōkan had at least once Zen disciple, Miwa Saichi (d. 1807), whom Ryōkan mentioned in a poem, he did not seem to make any effort to reach a large group of followers, and never passed on his dharma transmission.

Living outside the usual Zen monastic community, Ryōkan might have simply spent his life in relative peace and seclusion, and we would never have contemplated his existence or contribution to Zen. However, he became a well-known figure among the local villagers and a popular friend to village children, with whom he often played. Moreover, he exchanged poems with his brother, Yoshiyuki, as well as with other spiritually and poetically inclined figures of the day, including the Buddhist nun Teishin (1798-1872). Humble by nature, Ryōkan never compiled a collection of his poems in Japanese (although he did make a brief collection of his Chinese poems). But because he was so revered as a spiritual man, calligrapher and poet, the people with whom that he exchanged and gave poems reverently preserved them. As a result, over 1400 poems in Japanese and 450 poems in Chinese by Ryōkan have been recovered so far. The nun Teishin was the first to collect the poems in a volume titled *Hachisu no tsuyu* (Lotus Dew), dated 1835. Through these poems we have a wonderful sense of Ryōkan's spirit and his ability to paint his everyday encounters with a lyrical matter-of-factness rarely seen.

Bothered by Something

I shaved my head, became a monk,
plowed through the weeds, spent years looking for the Way.
Yet now wherever I go they hand me paper and brush,
and all they say is "Write us a *waka*!" "Write us a Chinese poem!"[3]

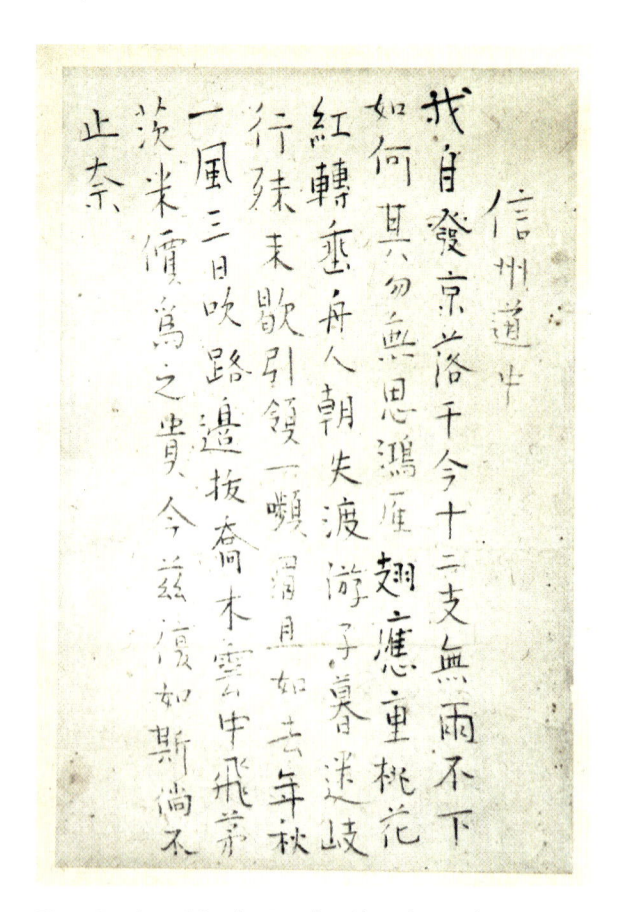

Fig 4: Ryōkan, "On the Road in Shunshū", Ink on Paper, 27.3 x 18 cm., Private Collection (reproduced with permission from Dr. Seo)

---

[3] Burton Watson, trans., *Ryōkan: Zen Monk-Poet of Japan* (NY: Columbia University Press, 1977), p. 111. A *waka* is a traditional Japanese-style poem.

[4] Stephen Addiss, 77 Dances: Japanese Calligraphy by Poets, Monks and Scholars 1568-1868 (Boston: Shambhala, 2006), p. 241-42.

In a Chinese-style poem written in 1795 or 1796, Ryōkan utilises his familiar light, open-style brushwork to reveal his concern over the weather and how it will potentially affect people (Fig. 4).

On the Road in Shinshū

Since I set out from the capital
Twelve days have gone by,
And not one of these has been without rain—
How can I help but worry?
Wings of wild swans and geese grow heavy,
Peach blossoms droop lower and lower;
Boatmen can't ply their morning ferries,
Travelers at evening lose their way.
It's impossible to halt my journey,
I crane my neck and knit my brows.
Will it be like autumn last year,
When the wind blew three days on end,
Huge trees were uprooted by the roadside,
And thatch from rooftops flew into the clouds?
Because of that the price of rice soared—
Will it be the same this year?
If these rains don't let up,
What? [4]

Is Ryōkan a maverick in the traditional sense? He lived outside the traditional Zen world, and as a result, never fought or rallied directly against it in any way. He left only one student that we know of, yet the legacy of his poems conveys the spiritual and everyday essence of Zen to a much broader audience than he could have ever imagined, revealing the purest aspects of the Zen mind, completely unfettered by institutional limitations.

Nantenbō Tōjū (1839-1925)

Experiencing the intense Westernization of Japan and anti-Buddhist sentiments of the Meiji Period (1868-1912), Nantenbō, more than any other monk, helped usher Zen securely into the 20th century. He did this largely by holding fast to traditional Zen values and being a fierce Zen teacher, who often ran into trouble for his independent spirit. Nantenbō trained under 24 Zen masters around Japan in order to achieve mastery of both the Inzan and Takujū lines, the two main teaching lineages within the Myōshin-ji school. Nantenbō trained numerous monks and served at several notable temples around Japan, but it was his relentless and staunch questioning and scrutiny of institutionalised Zen which made him a maverick. In 1879, when Myōshin-ji made plans to construct a large study center, Nantenbō vehemently protested, instead urging the building of a large training hall to produce truly disciplined priests who could better serve the country. Nantenbō also opposed the proposition of ranking priests by the incomes of their temple, thereby giving higher rank to priests of prosperous temples regardless of their spiritual accomplishments. Then in 1893, Nantenbō, proposed that all high-ranking Zen clerics should be tested on a standardised group of *kōan*, to prove their worthiness and credibility as Zen teachers. The inevitable bureaucratic repercussions and discourse manifest in this plan caused Myōshin-ji to reject it outright.

Like Hakuin, Nantenbō produced a huge body of paintings and calligraphies which were distributed among followers. In a particularly bold calligraphy which reads, "*Mumonkan*," meaning literally, "gateless gate," (Fig. 5) he refers to the famous collection of Zen *kōan* compiled in 1228 by the Chinese master Mumon (1183-1260, Ch. Wumen), but also suggests that the nature of Zen itself is both "gateless" and at the same time, not easily entered into due to the illusory nature of human thinking. While Nantenbō did countless scrolls utilising traditional Zen phrases and subjects, he, like Hakuin, also developed new, often rather personally inspired subjects. One of his most dramatic subjects is of a staff

Fig 5: Nantenbō, "Mumonkan" (1917), Ink on Paper, 67.2 x 32.7 cm., Chikusei Collection (reproduced with permission from Dr. Seo)

(*bō*, Fig. 6), a symbol often associated with Zen masters, and particularly with Nantenbō, who was famous for the *nanten* (nandina) staff he carried and from which he took his name. Nantenbō painted this subject numerous times, using it as a teaching tool and possibly as a reminder to the receiver of the image of Nantenbō's presence. The image is inscribed,

> If you speak, Nantenbō.
> If you don't speak, Nanten[bō].

While this reveals a clever reference to himself as a fierce teacher through the pun on his own name (Nandina staff), Nantenbō also makes reference to the traditional Zen phrase, "If he speaks, 30 whacks. If he doesn't speak, 30 whacks" made famous by the Zen master Tokusan (Ch. Te-shan, 782-865), who was known for using a big stick on his disciples. Moreover, Nantenbō has cleverly integrated word and image in this work, by completing the phrase, not with the written character for *bō*, but with the image of the large *bō*. Thus, word, image and Nantenbō's own presence are visually and spiritually intertwined.

While Nantenbō may have felt that his many suggestions and criticisms of Zen as an institution were ignored and dismissed, the very fact that he raised these issues and proposed new, innovative paths for the continued development of Zen training in the twentieth century is remarkable. Like Hakuin, Nantenbō worked to advance Zen during a rapidly changing Japan, while at the same time striving to preserve and protect its most deeply rooted spiritual traditions.

These Zen masters, each representing a different historical time and unique personal approach to Zen, all helped open Zen to the world. Nothing was off limits— they literally brought the here and now to a religion that espouses the practice of being in the here and now. Using poetry, calligraphy, painting, folk songs and everyday experiences, their unconventional visions and tenacious spirits took Zen out of its monastic confines to the world at large, and brought the world to Zen. Today, Shinzan Rōshi continues this lively untrammeled Zen tradition.

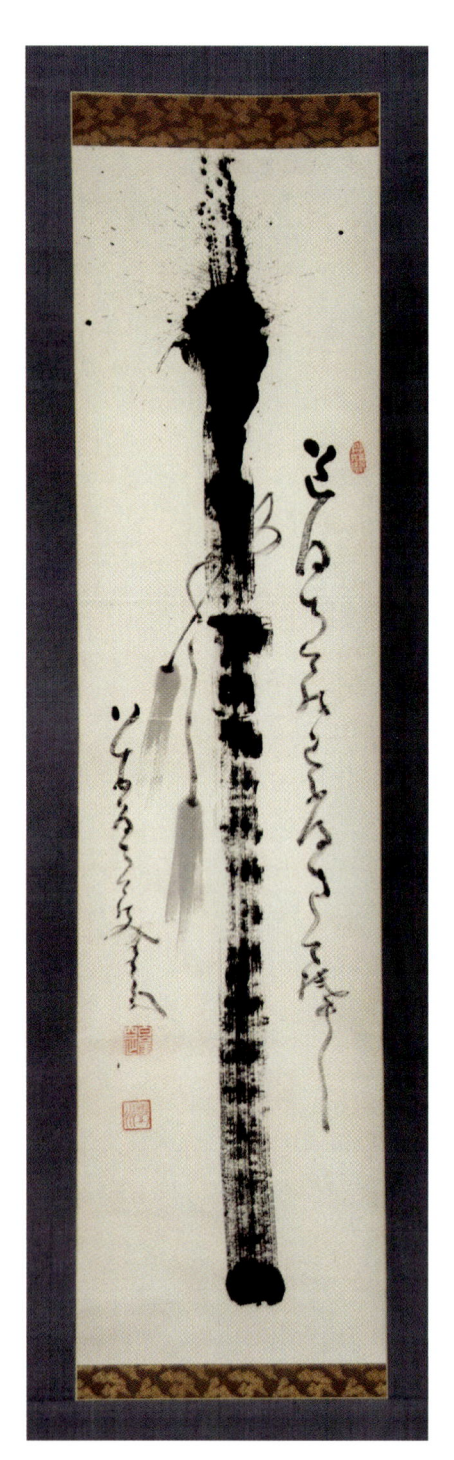

Fig 6: Nantenbō, "Staff" (1923), Ink on Paper, 33 x 127.5 cm., Private Collection (reproduced with permission from Dr. Seo)

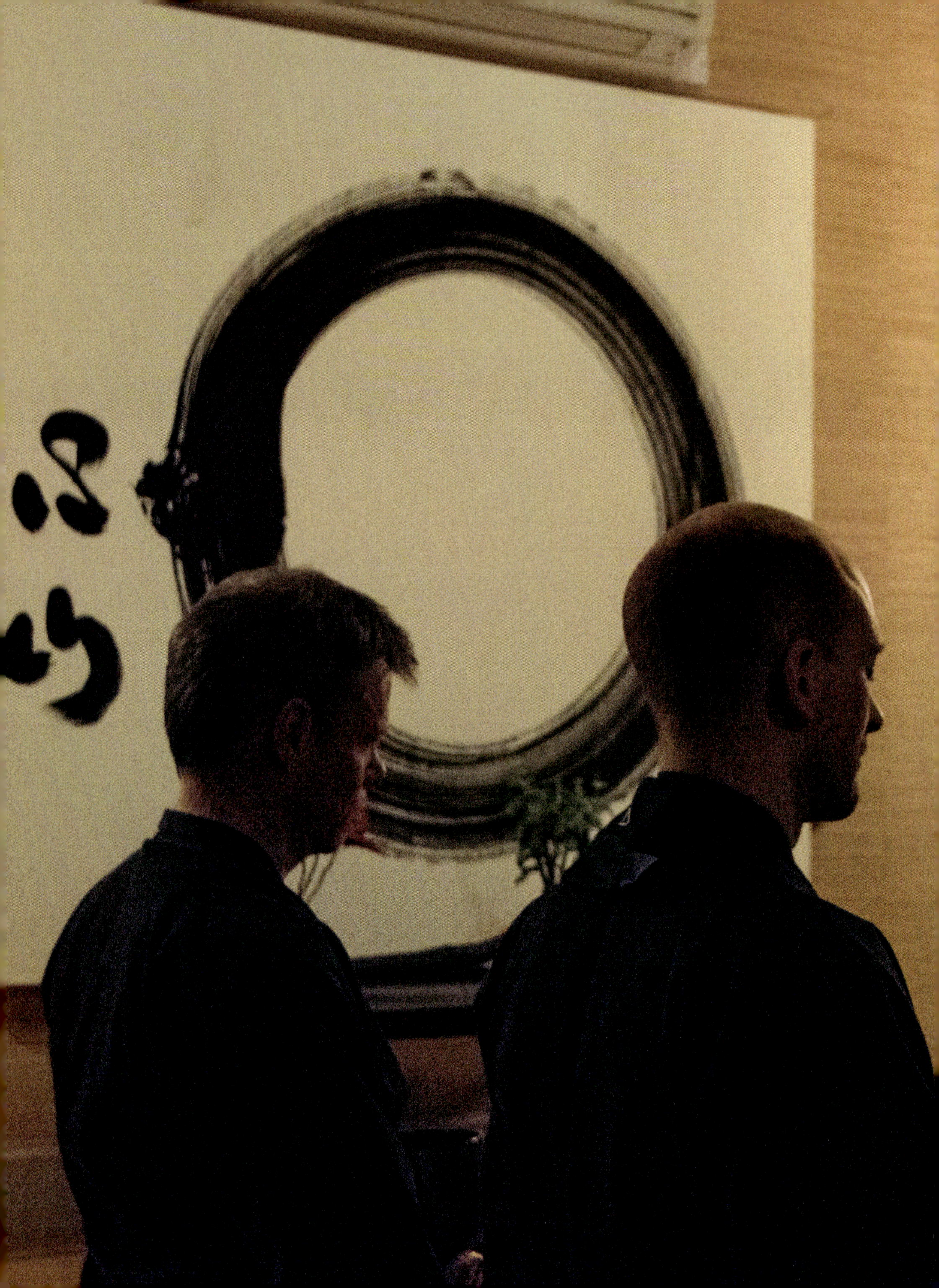

Zazen at Yugagyo Dōjō in Camberwell, London

CATALOGUE OF CALLIGRAPHIES BY SHINZAN RŌSHI

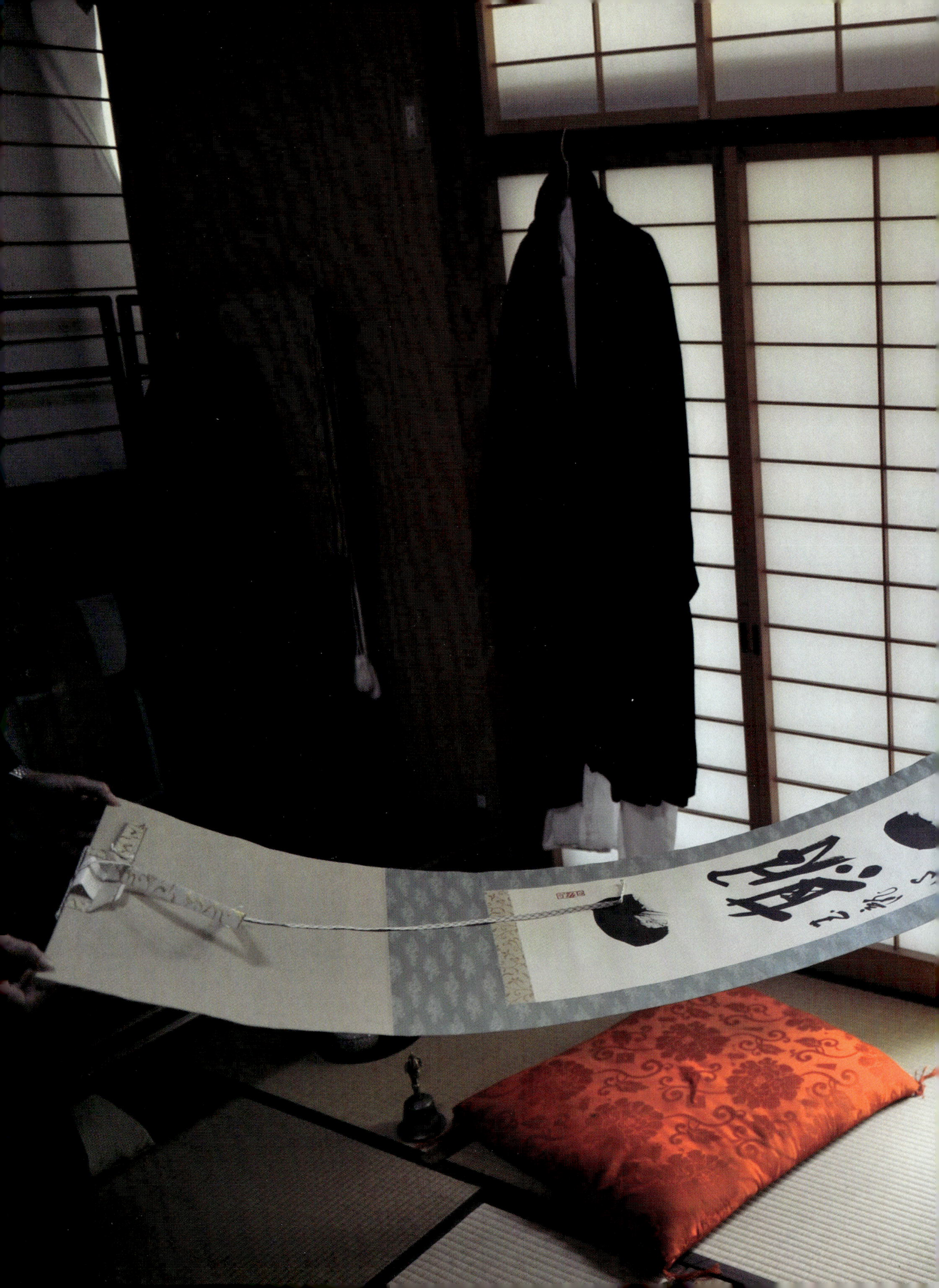

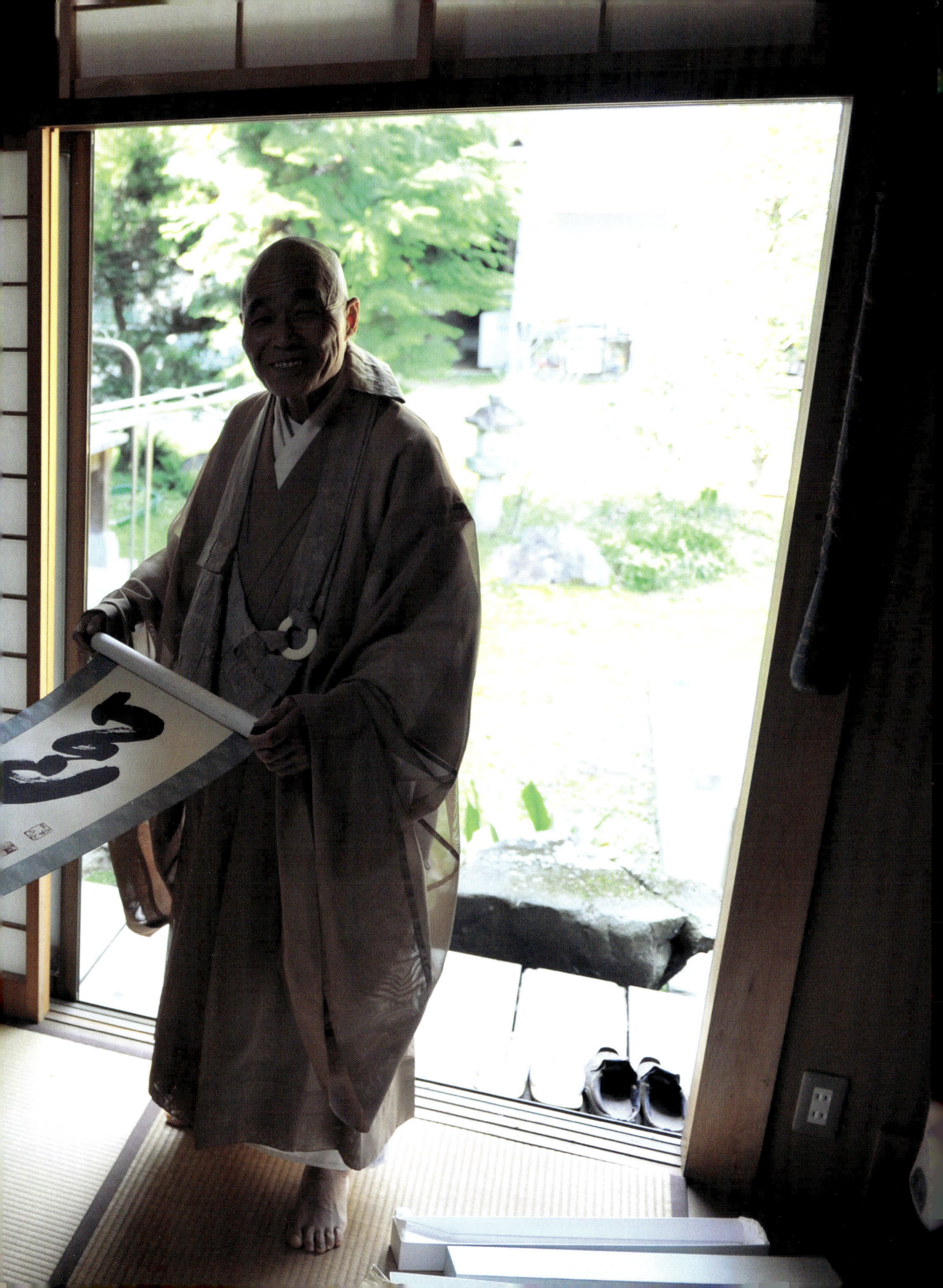

CATALOGUE CONTENTS

INTRODUCTION BY JOHN STEVENS 40

COMMENTATORS 42

ENSO (THE ZEN CIRCLE) 44
    Great *enso*: no inscription 44
    Enso: "See your own nature, become Buddha" (*Kensho jobutsu*) 48
    Enso: "Look at nature become Buddha" (in English) 50
    Enso: "Peace and harmony are most precious" (*Wa o motte totoshi to nasu*) 52
    Enso: "Don't forget to polish the jewel of your nature" (*Wasururu na shone tama*) 54

ONE-WORD BARRIERS 56
    "Barrier" (*Kan*) and maple leaves 56
    "Emptiness" (*Ku*) 58
    "Nothing" (*Mu*) 60
    "Mindfulness" (*Nen*) 62
    "Dream" (*Yume*) 64
    "Waterfall" (*Taki*) 66

TWO-WORD TEACHINGS 68
    "No mind" (*Mu shin*) 68
    "Purify the mind" (*Sen shin*) 70
    "No self" (*Mu ga*) 72
    "The middle way" (*Chu dō*) 74
    "Moving Zen" (*Do zen*) 78
    "Unborn" (*Fu sho*) 80
    "Power of the Way" (*Do riki*) 82

ONE-LINE TEACHINGS 84
    "Unity of relative and absolute" (*Hen chu sho*) 84
    "Become completely" (*Nari kiru*) 86
    "Heart of awakening" (*Bo dai shin*) 88
    "See your own nature, become Buddha" (*Kensho jobutsu*) 90
    "Pure breeze, bright moon" (*Seifu meigetsu*) 92
    "One chance, one meeting" (*Ichi go ichi e*) 94

"Harmony, respect, purity, tranquility" (*Wa kei sei jaku*) 96
"A true person of no rank" (*Ichi-mui no shinnin*) 98
"The sun rises shining light on heaven and earth" (*Hi idete kenkon kagayaku*) 100
"No birth or death" (*Mu shoji*) 102
"Yoga practice" (*Yuga-gyo*) 104

LONGER PHRASES 106

"Within nothingness there are inexhaustible treasures" (*Mu ichi motsu chu mujinzo*) 106
"Spring enters [the] thousand forests — here [and] there, warblers" (*Haru was senrin ni iru shosho uguisu*) 108

ZENGA – DARUMA 110

Daruma: "Pointing directly to the heart/mind, see your own nature, become Buddha" (*Jikishi ninshin, kensho jobutsu*) 110
Daruma: "Don't know" (*Fushiki*) 112
Daruma: "Seven times down, eight times up" (*Nana korobi ya oki*)............................... 114

ZENGA – KANNON 116

Kannon: "An unlimited ocean of good fortune and longevity" (*Fukuju kai mu ryo*)........... 116
Kannon: "The pure wisdom light (of Kannon) breaks through the darkness (of ignorance)" (*Fu ku sho jo ko, e nichi ha sho an*) 118

ZENGA – OTHER 120

Dragon staff: "A leisurely stroll under the blue sky" (*Senten heiho*)................................120
"Longevity" (*Ennen*) with pine 122

Introduction by John Stevens

The use of calligraphy and painting is one of the primary teaching vehicles of Zen Buddhism. It is well understood in the Zen tradition that contemplation of enlightened art fosters awakening no less than sitting in meditation, studying a sacred text, listening to a sermon, or going on pilgrimage. Proclaiming the Dharma with a brush and ink is as important, and effective, as proclaiming it with the spoken word, in sutras and texts, in chanting and ritual. One of the seals that Hakuin stamped on his brushwork read, "Paintings to liberate sentient beings." (Tibetan Buddhists say the same thing about *thangka* paintings: "Liberation through beholding.") Zen masters applied their insight to calligraphy and painting to challenge, inspire, instruct, and delight all those who choose to look.

In Zen brushwork, technique is important as a guideline providing structure and composition, but it is essentially just an aid. When a Chinese emperor asked a renowned calligrapher how to hold the brush he was told, "If your mind is correct then the brush will be correct." If one's mind is crooked or warped, so will be one's technique. When there is unity of brush, ink, paper and subject with the Buddha mind, the strokes come alive and the teaching imparted becomes vivid.

Shizan Rōshi's brushwork is anchored in the classical tradition of Zen art. This exhibition of his work displays all the central themes of Zen calligraphy.

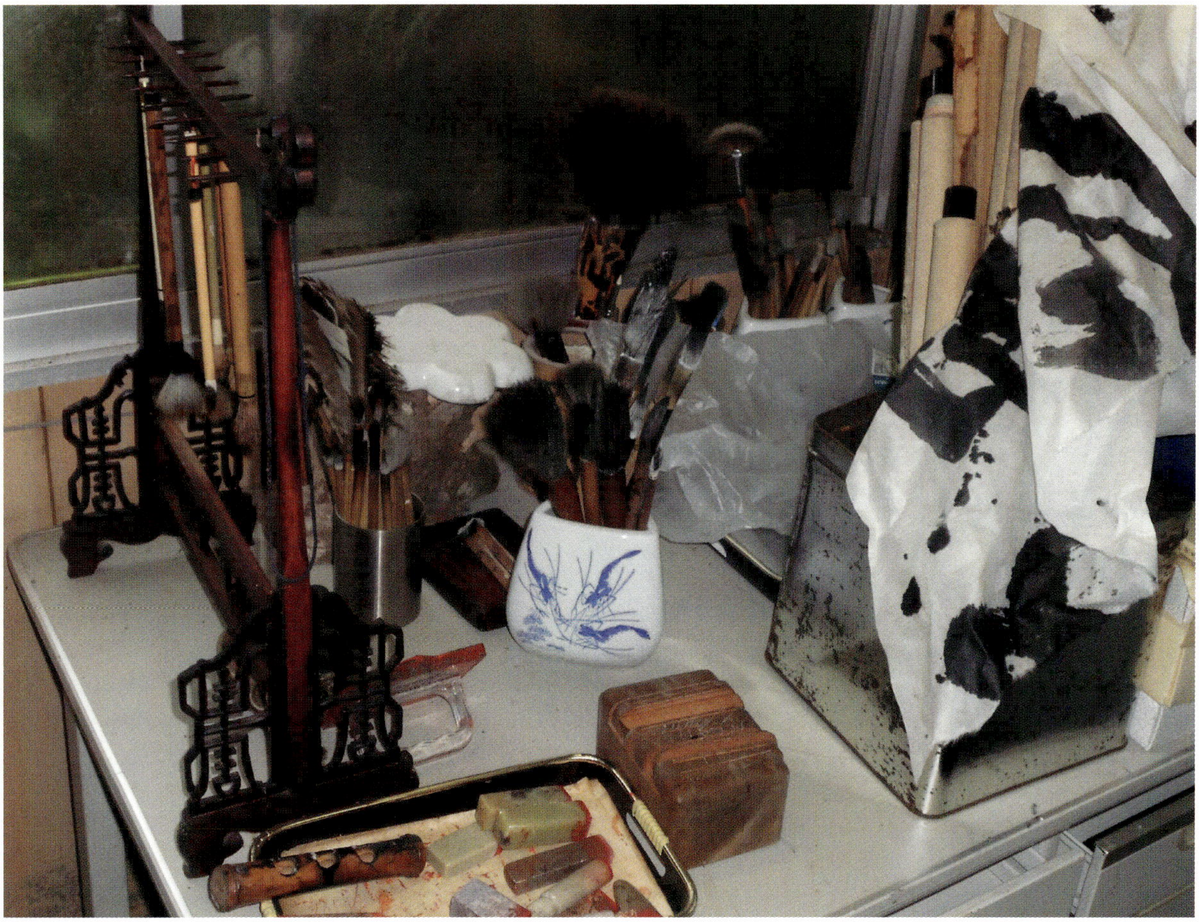

Commentators

John Stevens

John Stevens PhD (born Chicago, 1947) is a Zen Buddhist priest, teacher of Buddhist studies and aikido teacher. He is a retired professor of Buddhist Studies at Tohoku Fukushi University in Sendai, Japan. Stevens has written over thirty books on Buddhism, aikido and Asian culture. His works on Zen art include "Zen Brushwork: Focusing the Mind With Calligraphy and Painting", and "Sacred Calligraphy of the East". Stevens has curated several major Zenga (Zen art) exhibitions including "Zen Mind, Zen Brush: Japanese ink painting from the Gitter-Yelen Collection" for the Art Gallery of New South Wales, Sydney, "Enso: The Timeless Circle" for Buntin of Honolulu and "Zenga: Brushstrokes of Enlightenment" for the New Orleans Museum of Art..

Audrey Seo

Audrey Yoshiko Seo is an independent scholar of Japanese art. She received her PhD from the University of Kansas, and has since taught courses on Asian art and culture at the University of Kansas, University of Richmond, the College of William and Mary, and Virginia Commonwealth University. Her areas of research include Japanese Zen painting and calligraphy from the Edo period (1600-1868) through to the twentieth century, twentieth-century decorative arts, and contemporary Japanese fashion. She has curated several exhibitions and serves as a consultant for the Ginshu Collection of Zen paintings and calligraphy. Her publications and contributions include: "Adoption, Adaptation and Innovation: The Cultural and Aesthetic Transformations of Fashion," in "Since Meiji: Perspective on the Japanese Visual Arts, 1868-2000" (2011); "The Sound of One Hand: Painting and Calligraphy by the Zen Master Hakuin" written with Stephen Addiss (2010); "Enso: Zen Circles of Enlightenment" (2007); "Printed Moments: the Woodblock Imagery of Kamisaka Sekka," in "Kamisaka Sekka: Rimpa Master – Pioneer of Modern Design" (2003); "Fukushima Keido: Reflections in Ink" in "Zen no Sho" (2003); "The Art of Twentieth-Century Zen: Paintings and Calligraphy by Japanese Masters" written with Stephen Addiss (1998).

Enso (the Zen circle)

Great *enso*: no inscription

Paint on canvas, 175x175cm

Commentary by John Stevens

The symbol supreme of Zen art is the *enso*, a circle. From the beginning of Buddhism, enlightenment has been compared to the "bright full moon" and "a great round mirror." An *enso* can be interpreted as symbolizing: everything, nothing, infinity, eternity, perfection, enlightenment, the moon, mind, heart, centre, a rice cake, a fist, a frying pan, the top of a bucket, a bald head. *Enso* are truly timeless. From an art historical standpoint, most pieces can clearly be assigned to some period—Song Dynasty, Italian Renaissance, American Pop. With an *enso* painting, on the other hand, it is difficult to tell if it was brushed in the 13th century or the 21st.

Commentary by Audrey Seo

Enso are generally accompanied by an inscription that provides some suggestion of what the artist is trying to capture or say. *Enso* are often likened to the moon or a rice cake. Here Shinzan Rōshi has chosen to leave any concrete perceptions of the circle's meaning for the viewer to ponder. Some *enso* are accompanied by the phrase "*kore nan zo*" ("what is this?"), which directly challenges the viewer to consider the possibilities.

This question is not simply laziness upon the part of the artist, it comes from a poem by the Chinese Zen master Panshan Baoji (Jp. Banzan Hoshaku, 720-814 CE), a disciple of Baso Doitsu (Jp. Mazu Daoi, 709-788 CE):

> The perfect circle of the mind-moon is alone.
> Its light swallows ten-thousand things.
> The light does not illuminate objects.
> Neither do objects exist.
> The light and objects both cease to exist.
> What is this?

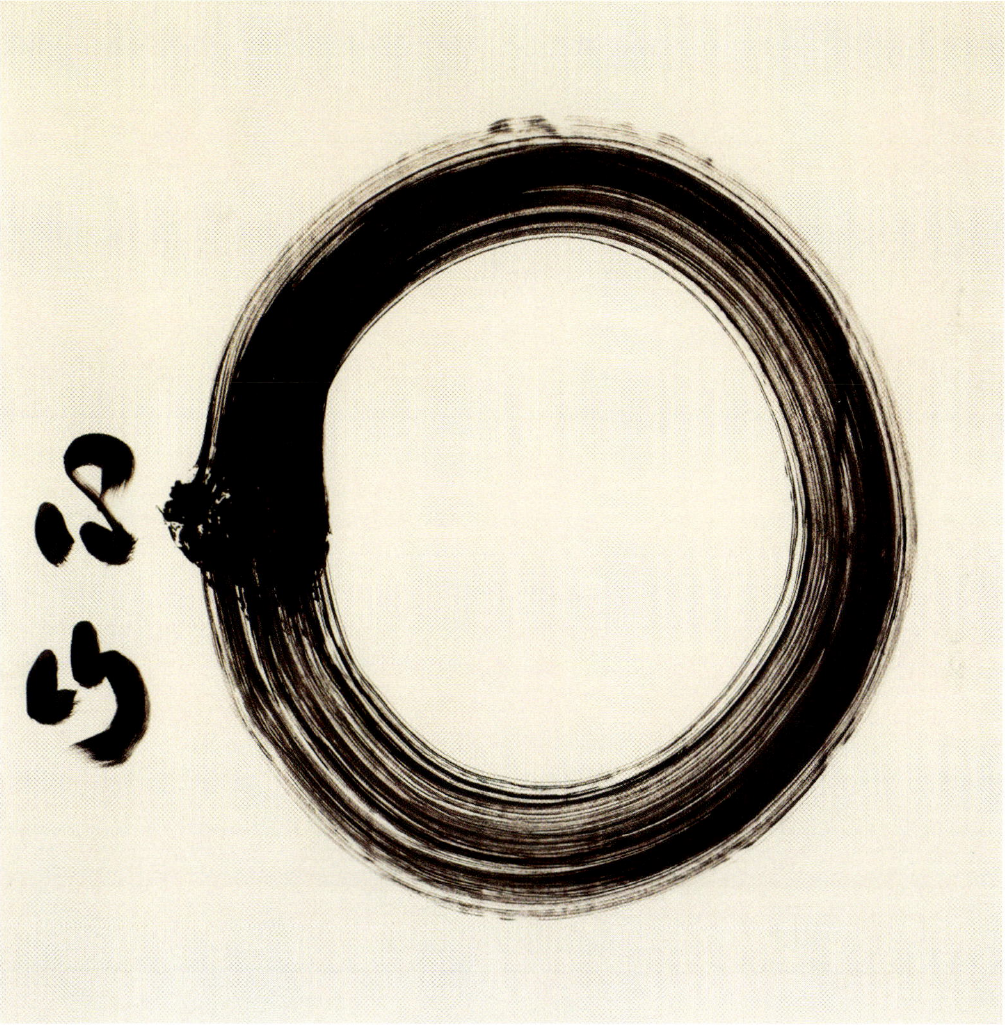

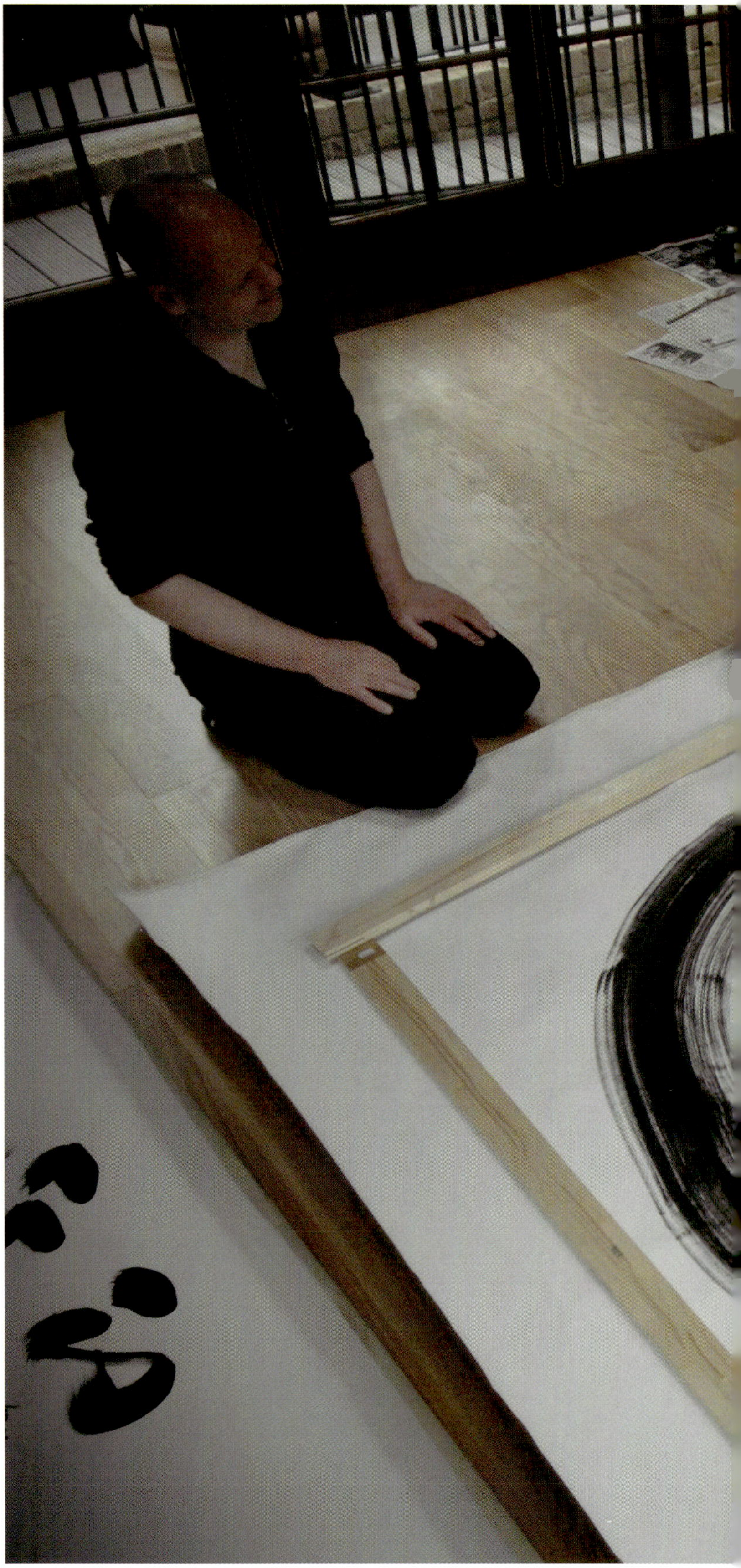

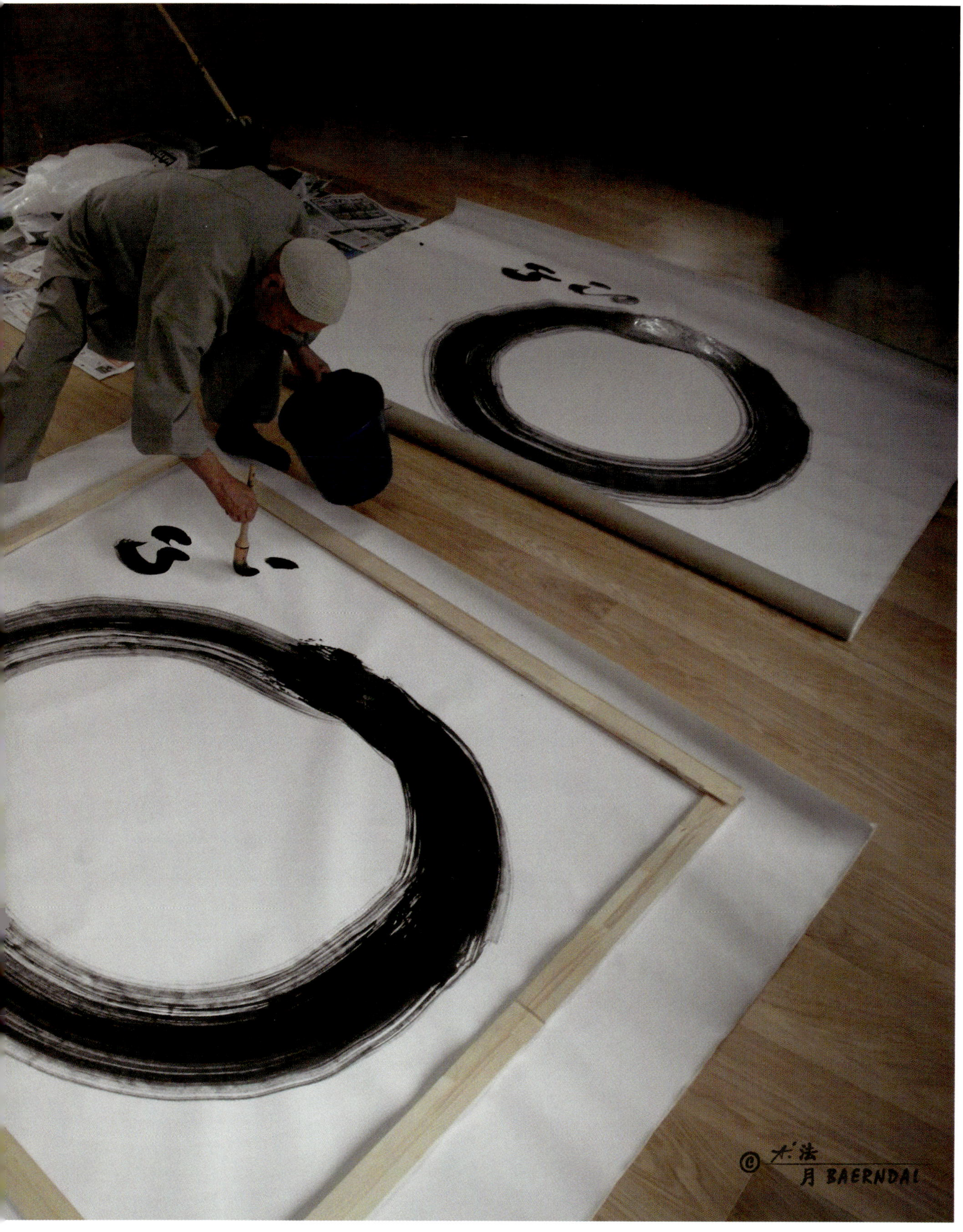
© 月 BAERNDAL

Enso: "See your own nature, become Buddha" (*Kensho jobutsu*)

Hanging scroll, 185x82cm

Commentary by Audrey Seo

Within this charming *enso*, Shinzan Rōshi has written "*kensho jobutsu*", "See your own nature, become Buddha"—a phrase attributed to Daruma. There is no point in looking to outside influences, one must look into one's own nature, only then will your true Buddha nature emerge. The work reveals the directness of the statement, framing it within a beautifully brushed circle of rich and varied ink tones.

While westerners often think of circles as being perfectly round, the wonderful nature of *enso* is often found in their imperfections, as in this one, which tilts slightly to one side, adding to its personality, uniqueness and presence.

49

Enso: "Look at nature become Buddha" (in English)

Hanging scroll, 150x82cm

Commentary by Audrey Seo

Zen has become one of the most universally known religions, and the term "Zen" has even developed marketing and social associations in the west beyond spiritual practice. Embracing this universal quality, Shinzan Rōshi has inscribed this *enso* in English, reaching out to all who might be curious. *Enso*, Zen circles, have also captured the imagination of westerners and found their way into the visual language of the west.

Enso are symbols of teaching, reality, enlightenment and myriad things in between. Seemingly perfect in their continuity, balance and sense of completeness, and yet often irregular in executions, *enso* are at once the most fundamentally simple and the most complex shape. They seem to leave little room for variation, and yet in the hands of Zen masters, the varieties of personal expression are endless. *Enso* evoke power, dynamism, charm, humour, drama and stillness. How and why is such a simple shape used to convey the vast meanings and complexities of Zen?

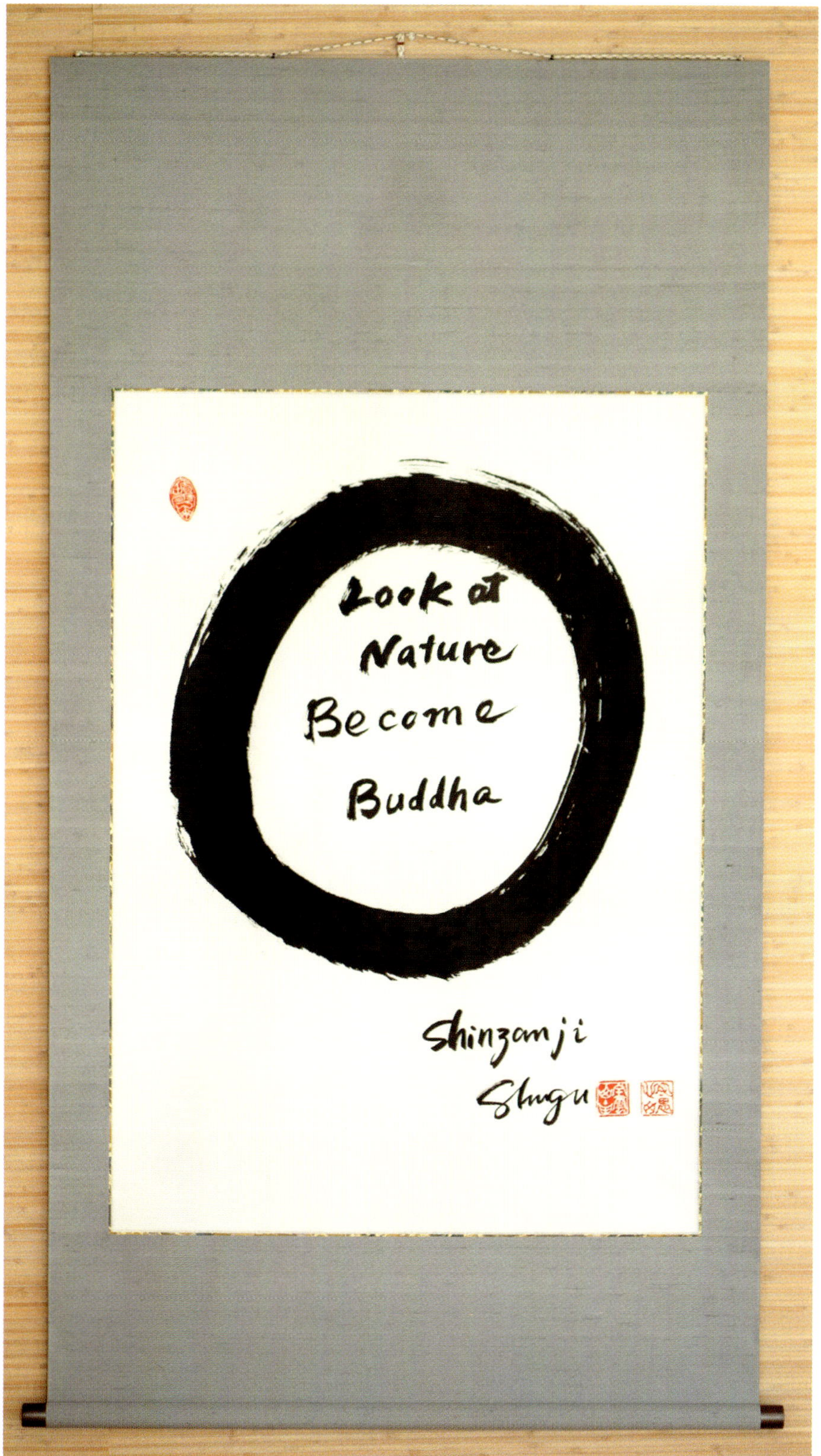
Look at
Nature
Become
Buddha
Shinzanji
Shugu

Enso: "Peace and harmony are most precious" (*Wa o motte totoshi to nasu*)

Hanging scroll, 110x65cm

Commentary by Audrey Seo

Shinzan Rōshi brushes a simple, elegant "*enso*"—a symbol of unity and harmony—and adds a traditional Japanese phrase that sums up a universal ideal, regardless of religious practice. In 604, the Japanese prince, Shotoku Taishi (572-622), composed his *Seventeen Articles*, emphasising social harmony among the classes,

> For all men have hearts, and each heart has its own leanings. Their right is our wrong, and our right is their wrong. We are not unquestionably sages, nor are they unquestionably fools. Both of us are simply ordinary men. How can anyone lay down a rule by which to distinguish right from wrong? For we are all, one with another, wise and foolish, like a ring which has no end ...
>
> Wm Theodore de Bary, ed. *Sources of Japanese Tradition, Volume 1*. NY: Columbia University Press, 1964, p50

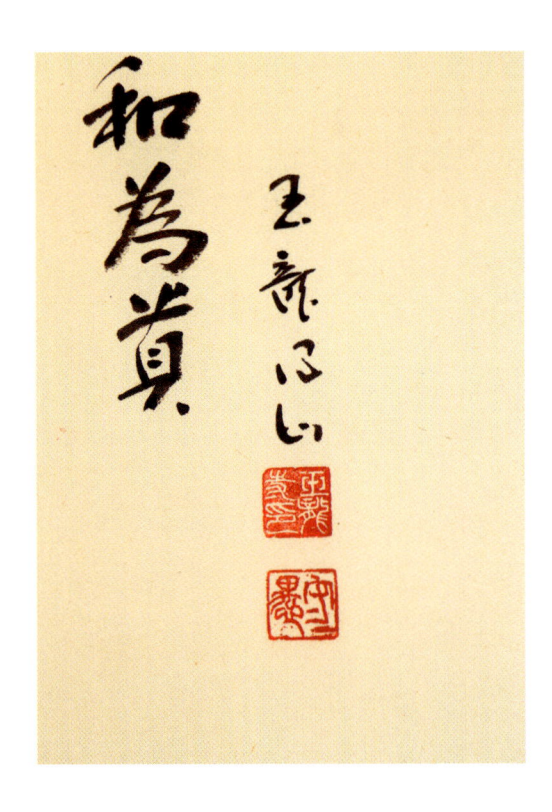

以和為貴

Enso: "Don't forget to polish the jewel of your nature" (*Wasururu na shone tama*)

Card shikishi, 27x24cm

Commentary by Audrey Seo

This *enso* displays beautiful examples of "flying white", where the white of the paper breaks through the dark rich ink, giving depth and energy to the brushwork. The circle is enhanced by the dancing characters surrounding it, which remind us to remember to continuously cultivate our true Buddha nature.

性れ玉　えるな

しんざん

One-word Barriers

"Barrier" (*Kan*) and maple leaves

Hanging scroll, 120x65cm

Commentary by Audrey Seo

Shinzan Rōshi has juxtaposed the rather foreboding character "*kan*" against the soft leaves of an autumn maple. Barriers in Zen are viewed as the numerous and varied obstructions that occur on the path towards enlightenment. These barriers can be represented by worldly illusions and attachments that must be broken down and discarded, or they can be aspects within Zen training that are established to help practitioners break through dualistic logic.

Kōans are often referred to as "*kan*" because practitioners must penetrate them to progress in their training.

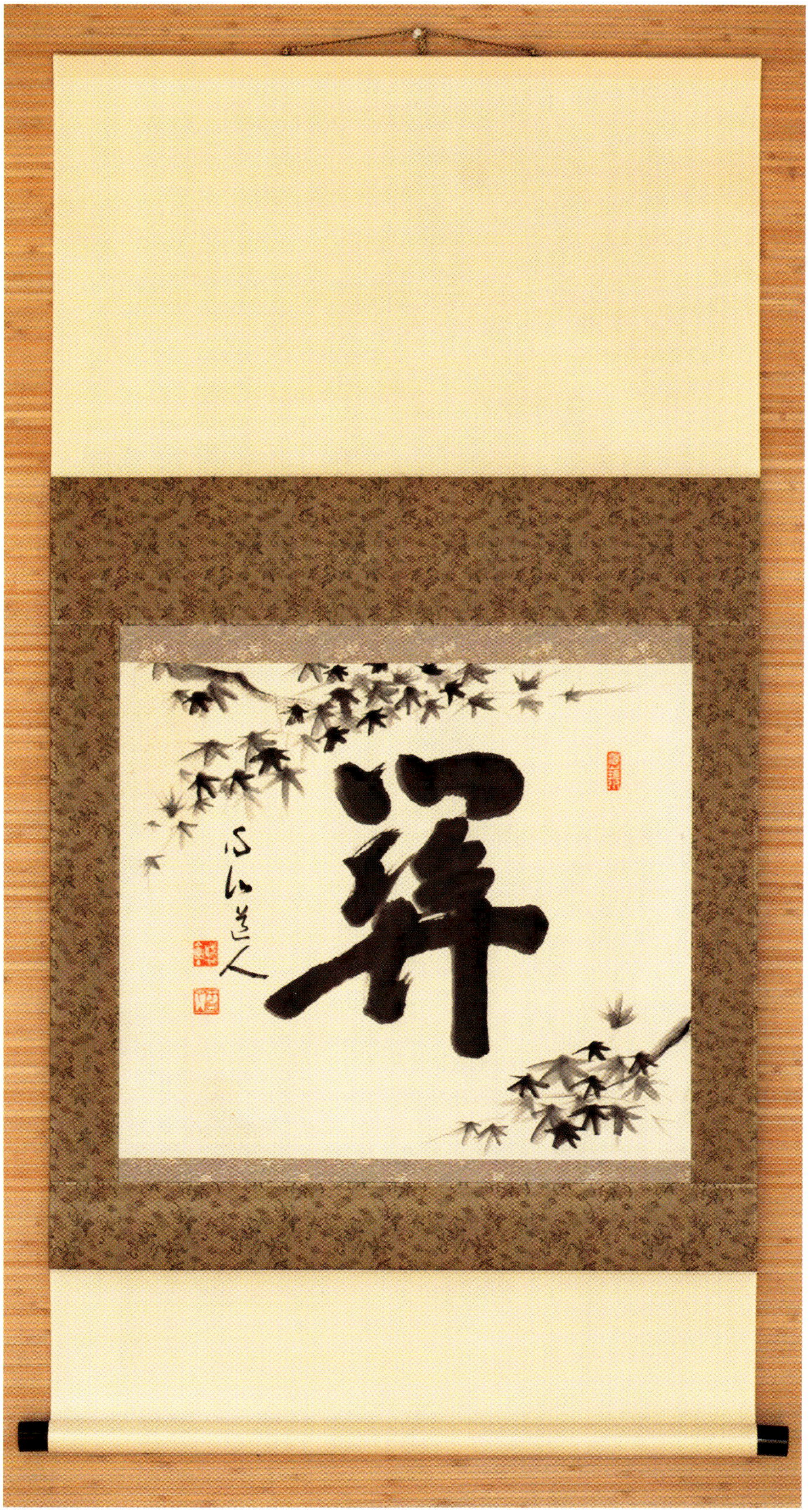

"Emptiness" (*Ku*)

Hanging scroll, 120x45cm

Commentary by Audrey Seo

From the Sanskrit "*śūnyatā*", "*ku*" refers to the central Buddhist notion of emptiness or the void. In Mahayana Buddhism, all things are seen as having no essence, empty of self-nature. This is not to suggest that things are non-existent—simply that all phenomena are merely appearances that are able to develop through the existence of "*ku*". The character also literally means "sky", which further reflects the expansiveness and vastness of the ideal.

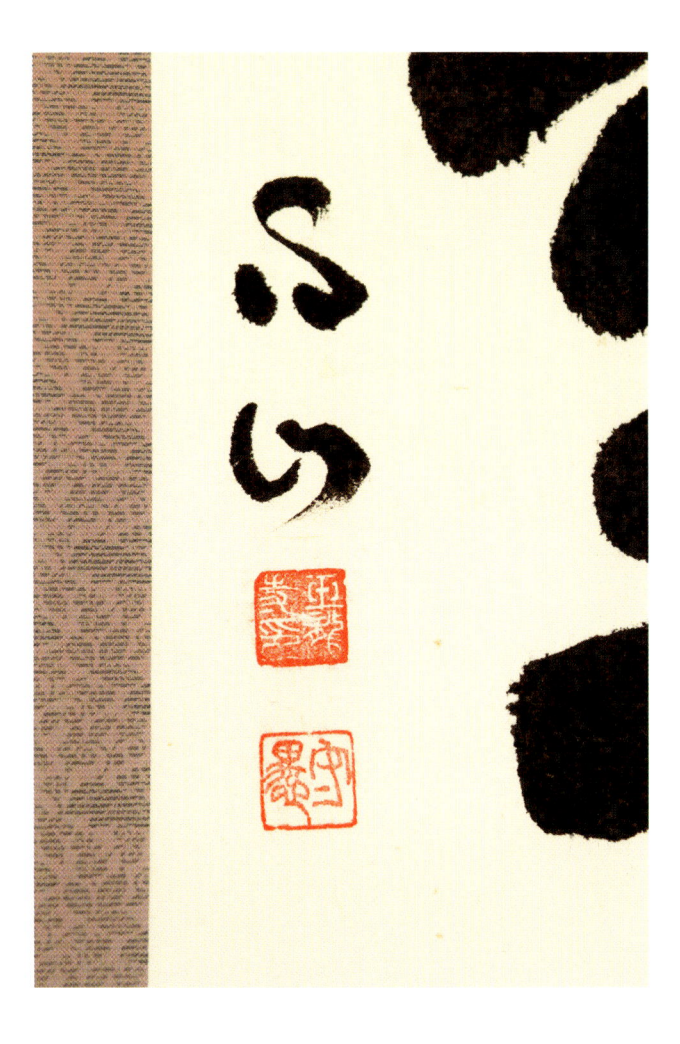

空

"Nothing" (*Mu*)

Card shikishi, 24x27cm

Commentary by Audrey Seo

"*Mu*" is referred to in the central *kōan* of Zen training, "Jōshū's Mu" in which a monk asks the Zen master Jōshū if a dog has the Buddha nature, to which Jōshū simply replies, "*Mu*"—neither an affirmative nor a negative. This *kōan*, case 1 in the *Mumonkan*, is usually one of the first given to novice monks as they begin their training. For many Zen practitioners "*mu*" represents the central barrier in Zen practice and is, in fact, often referred to as the "gateless barrier of Zen".

The character *mu* (無) is highly structured and balanced, it is a weighty character visually as well as philosophically. Here Shinzan Rōshi enlivens the character by emphasising its beautiful angles through his dramatic brush gesture. While he has simplified the structure of the character by using a running style of brushwork that links individual strokes into a single gesture, he maintains the balance and general integrity of the character's shape.

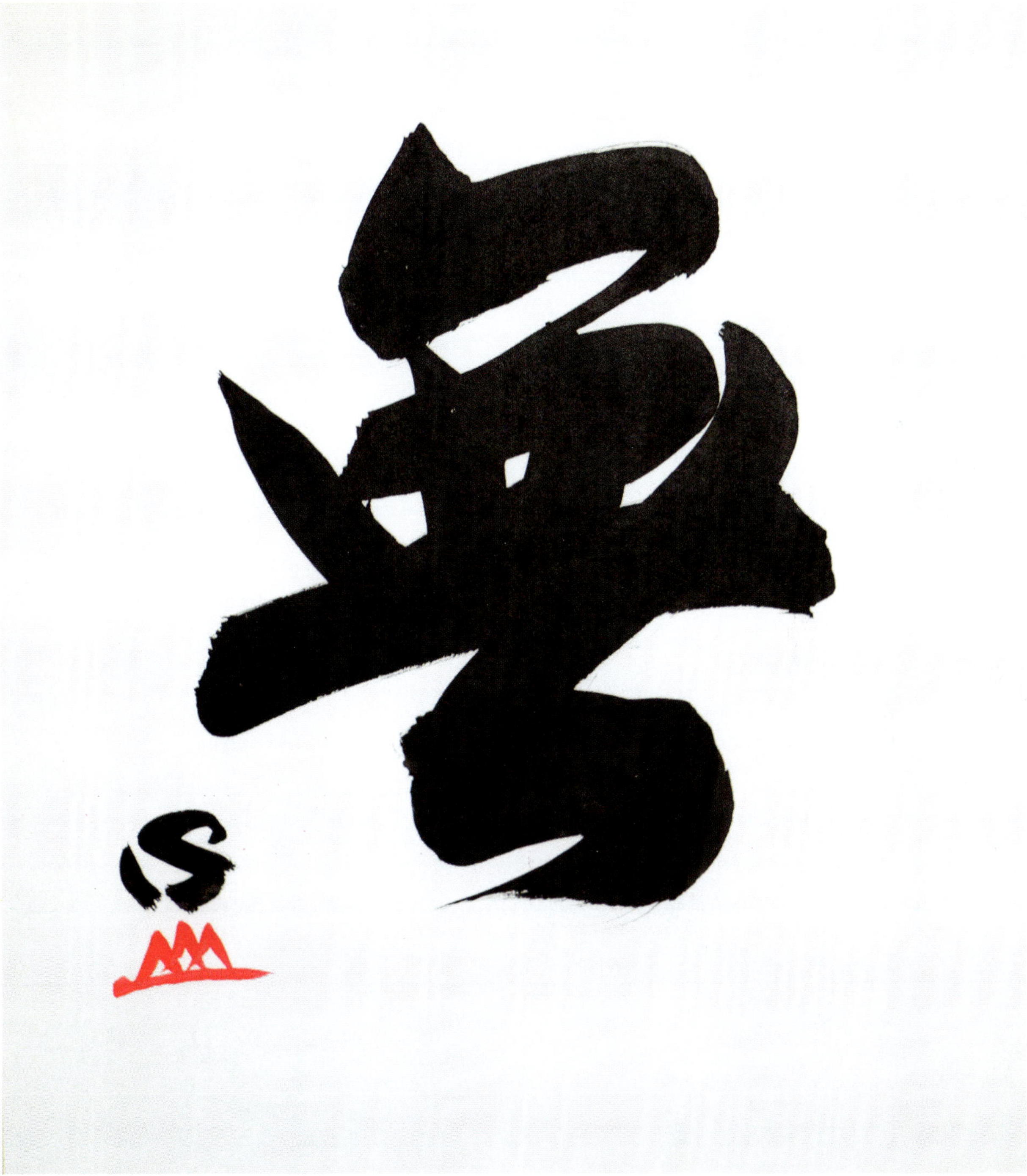

"Mindfulness" (*Nen*)

Card shikishi, 24x27cm

Commentary by Audrey Seo

The word "*nen*" ("mindfulness") seems simple and direct, yet it is one of the most complicated and difficult terms in Buddhism to define and discuss. In the most basic sense, it suggests the activity and constant presence of mind that one seeks as a part of Buddhist practice. Visually, the character (念) comprises two parts, the upper portion (今), which is translated as "now," and the lower portion (心), which means "heart/mind". So the character suggests the heart/mind being present in the moment. However, this is rather simplistic because it is also a matter of what your heart/mind is doing in the moment that is also a factor. Perhaps the truest way to be mindful is to follow the Buddha's *Eightfold Path*.

Shinzan Rōshi's rendering of "*nen*" is wonderfully dynamic with its sharp angles and terse brushstrokes. While mindfulness may suggest a quiet pensiveness, this calligraphy reminds the viewer to also be actively and energetically aware.

Shinzan Rōshi in his workshop at Gyokuryuji

念

"Dream" (*Yume*)

Hanging scroll, 170x45cm

Commentary by Audrey Seo

The character "*yume*" (dream) was a favourite among many Zen masters to write, and probably reflects the illusory nature of life that Zen seeks to understand. This idea is closely related to and in fact, may be borrowed from the Taoist tale in which Chuang-tzu dreams peacefully that he is a butterfly flying happily around. When he awakens, Chuang-tzu is not sure if he dreamt he was a butterfly or if the butterfly dreamt it was Chuang-tzu. Thus, the idea of distinctions is raised.

Shinzan Rōshi has written the character 夢 "dream" in a number of separate scrolls and, while initially the works all seem quite similar, in fact there are slight variations in the structure of his brushwork. In one work, the upper portions of the character, in particular the rectangular box with the two vertical lines going through it, are much more distinct, giving the character more structure and a sense of architectural stability. In another work, the upper portion of the character is deconstructed, the shapes simplified into a more fluid sweep of the brush.

These are the types of variations within calligraphy that make the art so captivating. Even within the work of one person, the possibilities for transforming characters are endless.

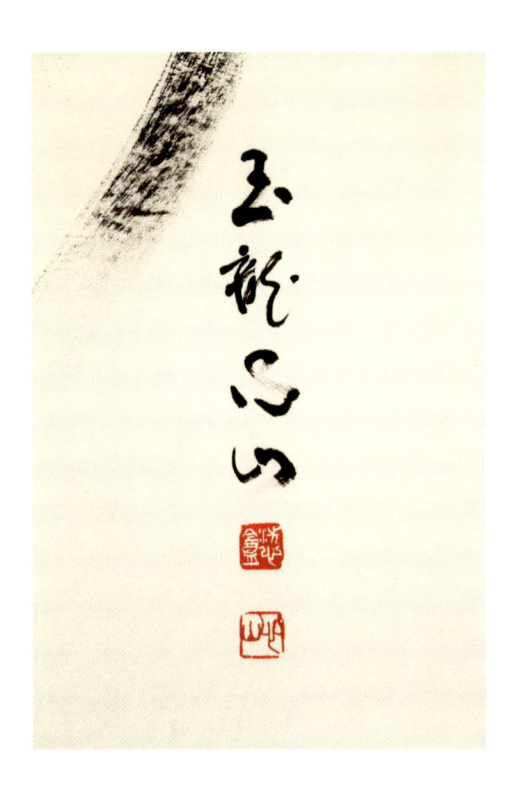

夢

"Waterfall" (*Taki*)

Hanging scroll, 190x45cm

Commentary by Audrey Seo

Words and images have always been interrelated in east Asian culture. Chinese characters (later adopted by the Japanese) were originally derived from pictographs that were gradually modified and codified into a system of written words. Many of these standardised words still reveal traces of their pictographic origins, and Chinese and Japanese artists through the ages have artfully manipulated and played with these word-picture associations.

Here, Shinzan Rōshi has brushed the character for "waterfall" and enabled it to cascade down the paper like water rushing down the side of a cliff. The energy of the rushing water is enhanced by the somewhat rough brushwork accentuated by the areas of "flying white", where the white of the paper shows through the breaks in the ink.

Spiritually, waterfalls are of great importance in the native Japanese religion, Shinto, which believes that native deities (*kami*) reside in natural phenomena such as mountains, waterfalls and rocks.

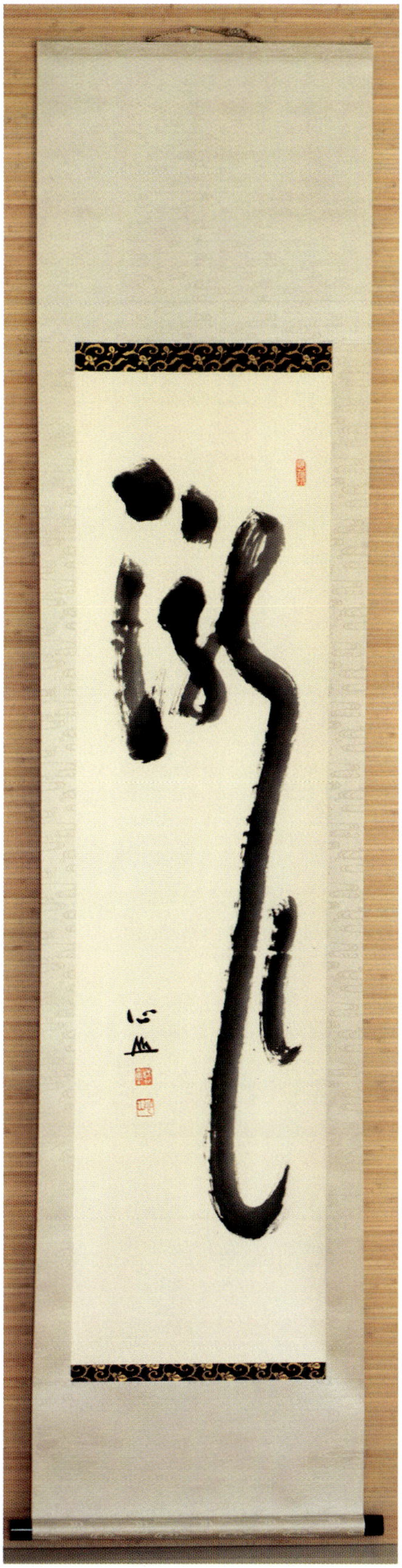

Two-word Teachings

"No mind" (*Mu shin*)

Hanging scroll, 140x45cm

Commentary by John Stevens

"*Mu shin*" is the key to Zen and the martial arts. The state of no-mind is free of discriminating thoughts, judgments, analysis, or preconceptions. In such a state, one acts naturally, freely, marvelously.

Commentary by Audrey Seo

Zen is the religion of "*mu shin*". The practitioner's goal is to achieve this state, in which all distinctions, ego, judgements and dualistic logic are removed. This does not leave an empty void, but instead a freedom of mind that is not fixed and is open to everything.

Shinzan Rōshi has explained in lectures that the idea of "no thought" does not mean the elimination of all thinking, but the end of all extraneous thinking. So, as he has pointed out, when you are thinking, then think with your whole being.

The juxtaposition of Shinzan Rōshi's characters is visually very interesting. The *mu* (無) is rather tight—its numerous strokes, particularly in its central section, melded together, and its various horizontal strokes compressed as if ready to spring. By contrast, the *shin* character (心) is open, displaying lots of negative space and breadth. It is interesting to compare this example of the character with the smaller version in Shinzan Rōshi's signature in the upper left.

無心

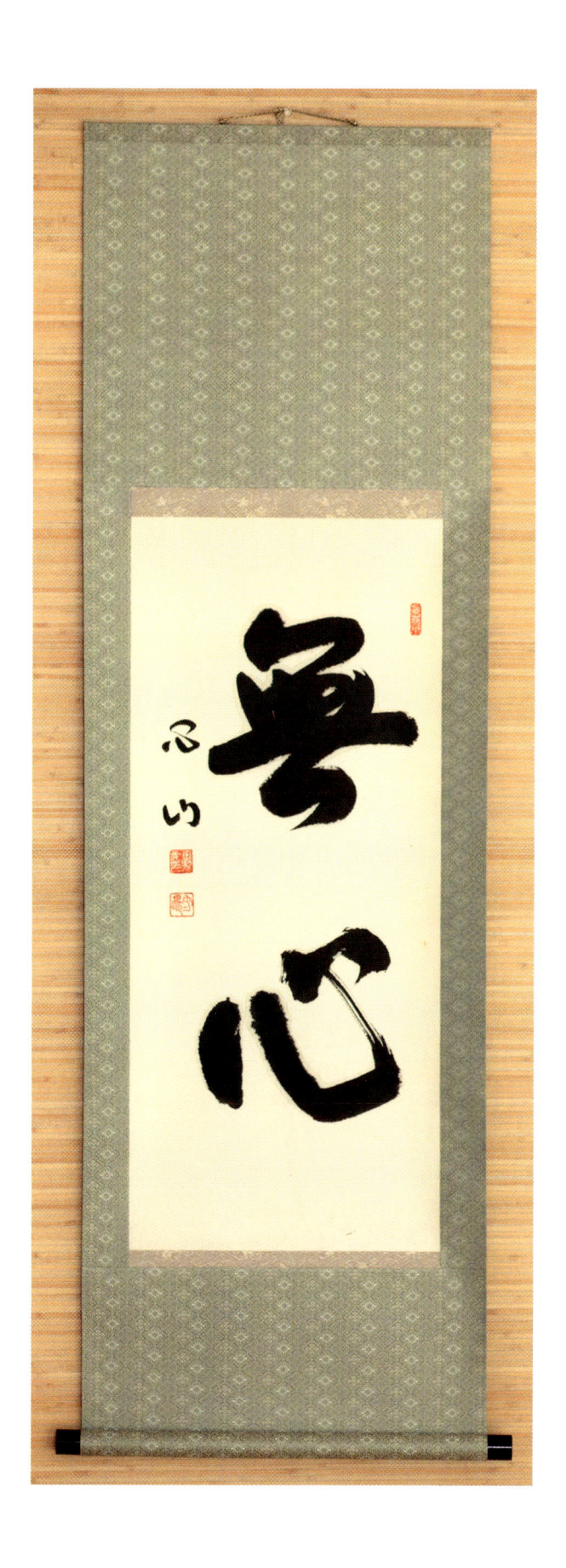

"Purify the mind" (*Sen shin*)

Hanging scroll, 135x65cm

Commentary by John Stevens

"Wash your Mind"—on occasion, our minds need to be purified, refreshed, and restored to its innate clarity.

Commentary by Audrey Seo

"*Senshin*" is known as one of the Five Spirits of *Budo* (Way of the Warrior). The Five Spirits are very closely related to basic Zen teachings. The Five Spirits of *Budo* are: *shoshin* (beginners' mind), *zanshin* (lingering mind), *mushin* (no mind), *fudoshin* (immovable mind) and *senshin* (purified mind). *Senshin* is a spirit that transcends the first four states of mind. It is a spirit of compassion that protects and harmonises the universe. It holds all life to be sacred, and reflects the Buddha mind. Fully embracing *senshin* is essentially equivalent to becoming enlightened and may well exceed the scope of daily aikido training.

Shinzan Rōshi has written these characters with a certain playfulness and freedom of spirit, reflecting the purified mind. The two characters (心洗) nestle next to each other, their individual spaces indistinguishable. In particular, the three dots that serve as the left-hand portion of the "*sen*" character, visually interact with the gesturally free "*shin*" character, which tilts casually to the left.

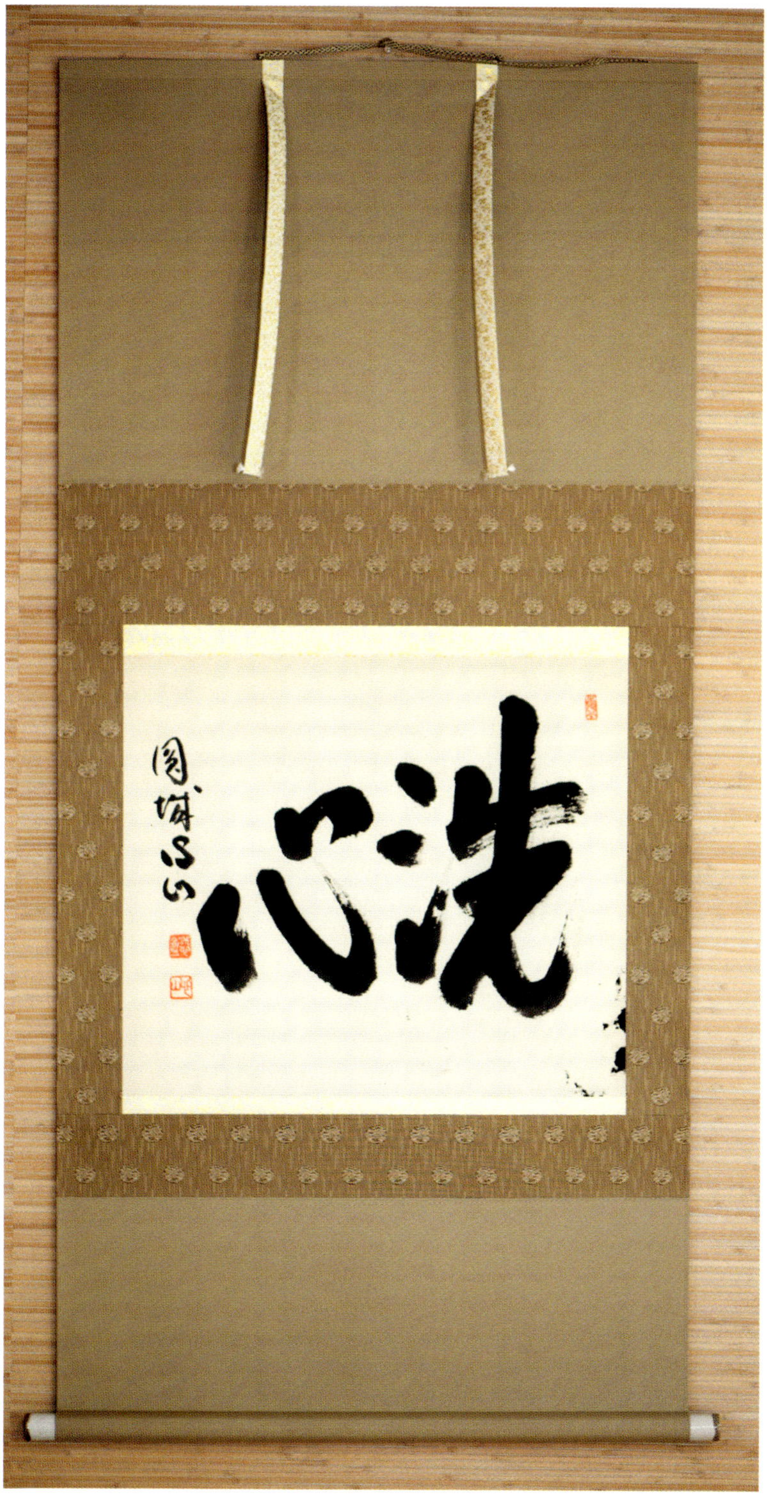
洗心

"No self" (*Mu ga*)

Hanging scroll, 140x45cm

Commentary by John Stevens

One of the fundamental principles of Buddhism is that there is no abiding "self" (*anatman*). Buddha himself said that understanding of *anatman* was the hardest nut to crack—it cannot be explained or even conceived intellectually. *Muga* is an experience, not a concept. In general Japanese conversation, *muga* is used in a more positive sense—"selflessness" as in "selfless love." This understanding of *muga* is also a Zen virtue.

Commentary by Audrey Seo

This is an idea similar to "*mu shin*" ("no mind"), in which one strives to remove one's sense of ego and the idea that one is a separate entity. By so doing, you can free yourself from worldly illusions and attachments, leading to an ultimate freedom of mind and self.

The characters here are brushed with an energy and freedom that reflects "no self". The balance of each character and dynamism of the various brushstrokes reveal a pure mind and lack of self-consciousness.

無我

"The middle way" (*Chu dō*)

Hanging scroll, 160x45cm

Commentary by John Stevens

The shortest definition of Buddhism. In Zen practice, *Chu dō* means "Stay in the Centre."

Commentary by Audrey Seo

The Middle Way sums up the essence of Buddhism. The historic Buddha, Shakyamuni, after renouncing his life as a prince, spent six years in the mountains as an ascetic. He eventually rejected this austere lifestyle, believing that there must be a way to attain enlightenment without exhausting one's body and mind. Shakyamuni descended from the mountains, emaciated and weak.

After being nursed back to health by the daughter of a cowherd, he regained the strength needed for his impending enlightenment. Despite being abandoned by his fellow ascetics for breaking his fast, and having his resolve tested, Shakyamuni sat in meditation under a pipal tree (the Bodhi tree) and eventually achieved enlightenment.

During his first sermon, Shakyamuni set forth the Four Noble Truths and the Eightfold Path. Most importantly, he reiterated the importance of the Middle Way, stating:

> "Ignorant people practice austerities; those who seek pleasures gratify their senses. As neither method leads people to liberation, these two extremes are utterly wrong; they are not the right ways.
>
> Devoting oneself to ascetic practices with an exhausted body only makes one's mind more confused.
>
> To indulge in pleasures is also not right; this merely increases one's foolishness, which obstructs the light of wisdom."
>
> William Theodore de Bary. *The Buddhist Tradition* NY: Random House, 1972, p71

Shinzan Rōshi reflects the importance of this basic teaching in this dramatic work in which he drags the central horizontal brushstroke of the first character, *middle*, down through most of the compositional space, and in effect, through the middle of the whole work.

中道

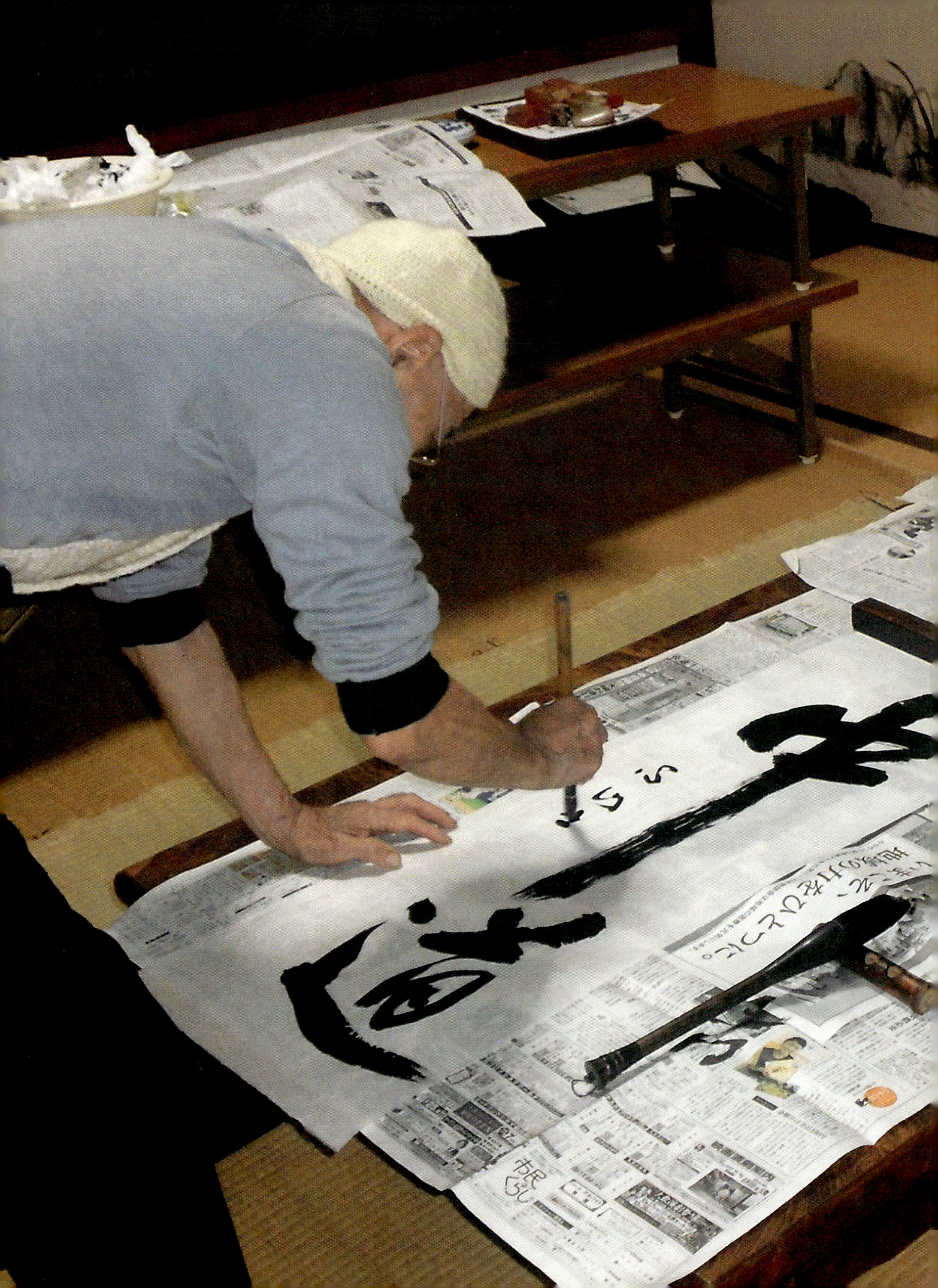

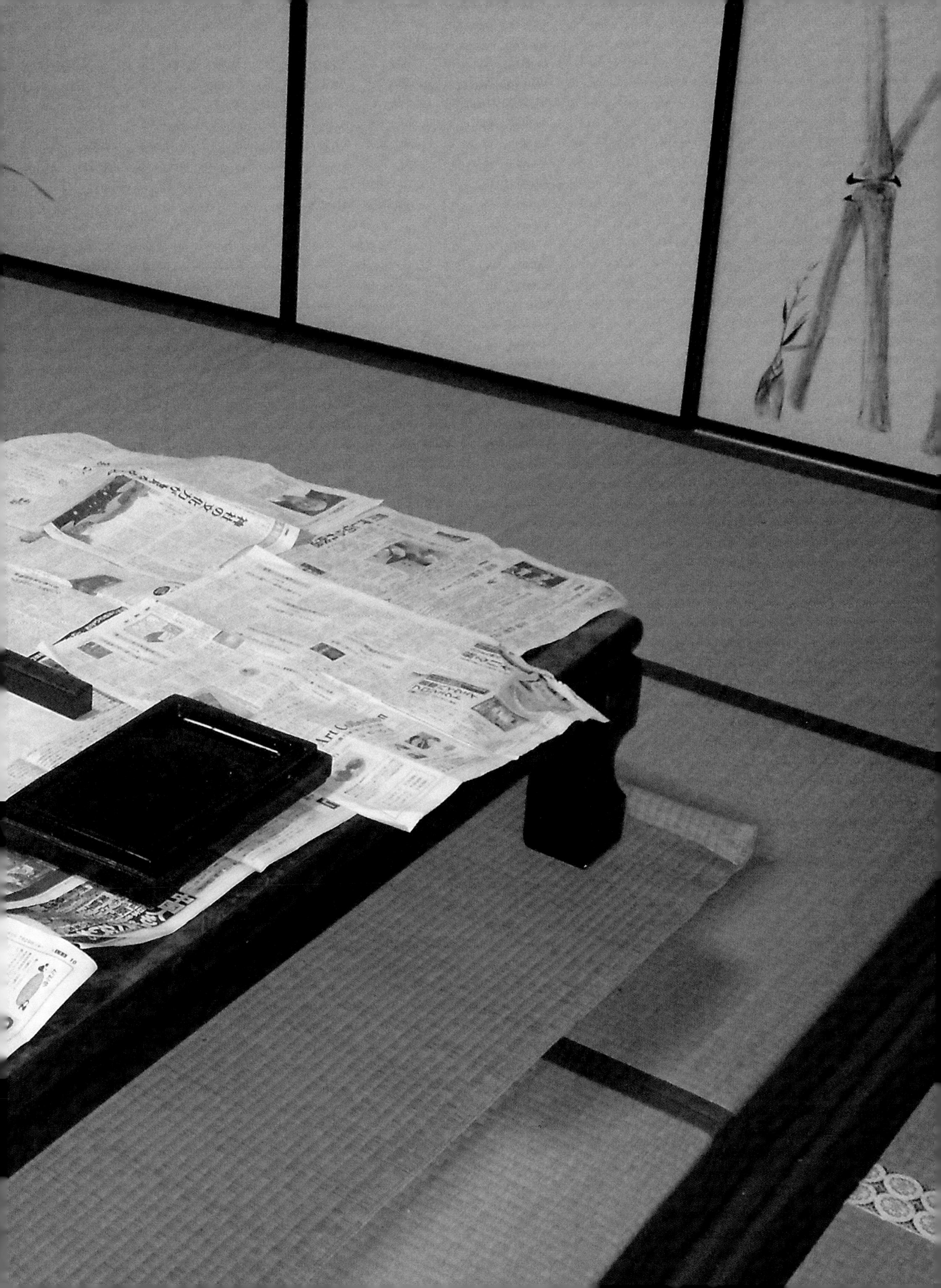

"Moving Zen" (*Do zen*)

Hanging scroll, 158x45cm

Commentary by John Stevens

The great Zen master Hakuin said "Meditation in action is a thousand times superior to meditation in stillness."

Commentary by Audrey Seo

"*Do Zen*" suggests the ideal of unifying physical strength and mental power, thus bringing the two into harmony. As a result, the term is often associated with *aikido*.

The dynamic energy and the aesthetic balance of the two characters juxtaposed against the bold structural stability of both characters reflects this philosophical harmony and the spiritual focus of the artist.

動禅

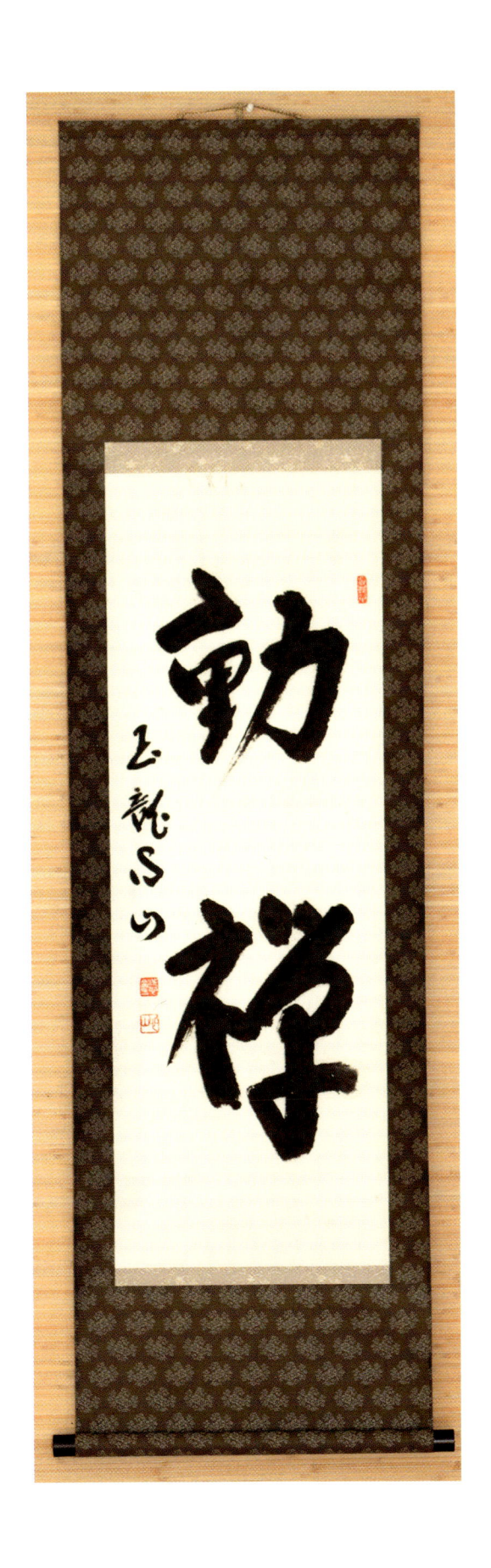

"Unborn" (*Fu sho*)

Hanging scroll, 145x40cm

Commentary by John Stevens

While this teaching is most closely associated with the Zen master Bankei, it is a key aspect of Shingon (Japanese Tantra) as well. Both teach that we should "Abide in the Unborn." The Unborn is perfect and complete. There is no special method needed other than to be oneself, totally natural and spontaneous.

Commentary by Audrey Seo

The Zen master Bankei (1622-1693) devoted much of his life to propagating his teaching of the unborn. He preached that vigorous Zen training would lead to a state which he called the state of the "unborn" ("*fusho*"). This state was the mind/heart in its purely unadulterated form. During an early bout of tuberculosis, Bankei resolved to die. He wrote of his experience:

> I felt a strange sensation in my throat. I spat against a wall. A mass of black phlegm, large as a soapberry, rolled down the side ... Suddenly just at that instant ... I realised what it was that had escaped me until now: all things are perfectly resolved in the unborn.
> Norman Waddell, trans., *The Unborn: The Life and Teaching of Zen Master Bankei*, 1622-1693. San Francisco, CA: North Point Press, 1984, p10

Fusho is also the first part of the phrase, "*fusho fushi*" ("no birth, no death"), which reveals the ultimate state of nirvana.

Shinzan Rōshi's two characters are bold, solid and direct. The strokes are evenly weighted in width and ink tone, achieving a beautiful balance. Yet he also leaves the tips of many of the strokes "open"—not perfectly rounded and closed—creating a sense of movement and energy. This is particularly evident in his diagonal strokes.

不生

"Power of the Way" (*Do riki*)

Card shikishi, 24x27cm

Commentary by Audrey Seo

The word "*do*" ("way" or "path") is probably one of the most familiar Chinese words to westerners, whether they realise it or not. The Buddha, Shakyamuni, promoted the following of the Middle Way, avoiding extreme acts of asceticism, as well as over-indulgence. In effect, practising Buddhism is following the Middle Way. But the term has also been adopted by other practices and activities that have become deeply associated with Buddhism or Zen. The most familiar include, *aikido* (way of the spirit of harmony), *bushido* (way of the warrior), *kendo* (way of the sword), *chado* (way of tea) and *shodo* (way of the brush). In general, following a path denotes a devotion to a highly developed and often ritualised form of practice, in art, martial art or spirituality. The term "*do riki*" reinforces this form of commitment and dedication.

While Shinzan Rōshi has written the first character, "*do*", in a slightly running style, the basic structure of the character is clear, and viewers will be able to pick this character out in other instances.

道力

はつの筆

One-line Teachings

"Unity of relative and absolute" (*Hen chu sho*)

Hanging scroll, 160x45cm

Commentary by John Stevens

The final level of Tozan's Five Ranks. Tozan's verse reads:
   Who can match one who does not fall into being or non-being?
   All human beings hope to escape from the ceaseless the flow of samsara
   But ultimately you must sit in the midst of this world's dust.

Commentary by Audrey Seo

This phrase represents one of the five degrees of enlightenment as established by the Chinese Zen master, Tung-shan Liang-chieh (807-869, Jp. Tozan Ryokai). Each level reflects an increasing depth of enlightenment. "*Hen chu sho*" (the second stage), literally represents "*sho*" (the absolute) in the midst of "*hen*" (the relative), the point at which the ideal of non-distinction emerges and the illusions of diversity and multiplicity recede. Here the character, "*chu*" (middle), is positioned between the other two characters, its strong vertical stroke linking the characters compositionally.

兼中到

"Become completely" (*Nari kiru*)

Hanging scroll, 140x45cm

Commentary by John Stevens

Zen is "*nari kiru*," a state of being, not an activity.

Commentary by Audrey Seo

Shinzan Rōshi often uses the term "*nari kiru*", which he translates as "becoming cut off". It is a way of emphasising the Zen ideal of being fully in the moment no matter what you are doing or feeling. An everyday example given by Daizan Rōshi is when you wash the dishes, you become 100% engaged in this activity.

This scroll is interesting because it combines the calligraphic aesthetics of the more complex Chinese characters (the first and third characters) with the more simplified, curvilinear Japanese *kana* characters, creating a unique rhythm and sense of space.

成り切る

"Heart of awakening" (*Bo dai shin*)

Hanging scroll, 140x45cm

Commentary by Audrey Seo

The determination to achieve enlightenment. This was an aspect of practice stressed by Zen master Dōgen (1200-1253) — that by having the pure resolve to find truth, one comes to understand that self is no greater than any other phenomenon. This then allows one to be open to a reality without being limited by one's self.

Shinzan Rōshi brushes these three characters with a powerful gesture that emphasises terse strokes and angular aspects of each characters, including the final "*shin*" character, which generally appears more rounded.

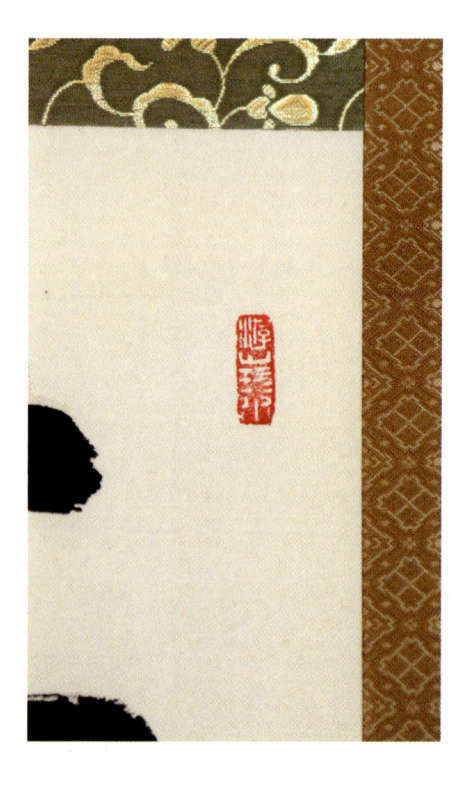

菩提心

"See your own nature, become Buddha" (*Kensho jobutsu*)

Hanging scroll, 140x45cm

Commentary by Audrey Seo

Perhaps the most direct phrase in Zen when considering one's own personal path. "See your own nature and become Buddha", is a phrase attributed to Daruma himself and inscribed often on Daruma portraits (this passage is found in the *Hsueh-mo lun*, a work attributed to Daruma, but actually of later origin). There is no point in looking to outside influences or effects—no use for texts, or idols. One must look into one's own nature—only then will your true Buddha nature emerge.

Shinzan Rōshi's script is clear and direct here, with each stroke of the brush individualised and succinct. Only in the final two characters, "become" and "Buddha", does he allow a few of the strokes to run together, creating a dramatic visual finish.

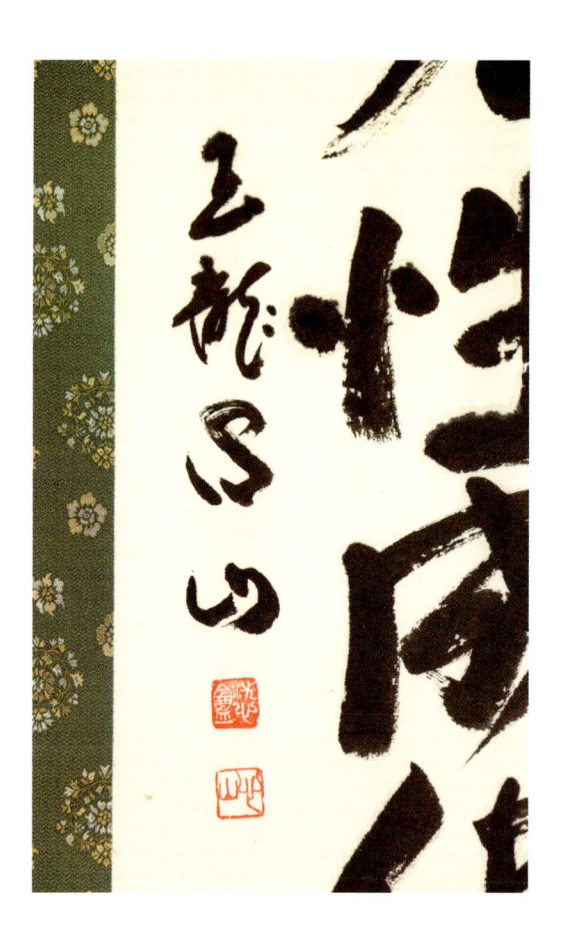

見性成佛

"Pure breeze, bright moon" (*Seifu meigetsu*)

Hanging scroll, 160x45cm

Commentary by John Stevens

A description of satori—to be refreshed and illumined.

Commentary by Audrey Seo

A beautifully poetic way to suggest the purity of enlightenment and lack of worldly illusions and distractions. The full phrase is often given as "*Meigetsu seifu wo harau*" ("The bright moonlight wipes away the pure breeze").

Visually, the lightness and fluidity of Shinzan Rōshi's calligraphic gesture suggest a pure breeze, while the dark, rich ink reveals an almost reflective quality.

清風明月

"One chance, one meeting" (*Ichi go ichi e*)

Hanging scroll, 186x45cm

Commentary by John Stevens

All our actions are right here, right now.

Commentary by Audrey Seo

This is a concept related to the ideal set forth in the tea ceremony. Roughly translated the phrase means "one chance, one meeting" or "one encounter, one opportunity". In other words, you have one opportunity to experience a particular interaction with someone or a particular moment—so do not waste it. The term reflects aspects of Zen concepts of transience, of being in the moment and fully experiencing that moment: if it is cold, be cold.

In the context of tea ceremony, "*ichi go ichi e*" reflects the idea that each tea meeting is unique, and can never be repeated in the same way again. Therefore, each gathering should be appreciated fully and completely. Even if you have the opportunity to meet the same person or people again, the experience will not be the same because it will reflect a different moment.

In his calligraphy, Shinzan Rōshi seems to emphasise the character for "one" ("*ichi*"), which appears as the first and third characters as horizontal strokes, visually focusing on the singularity of the moment and experience.

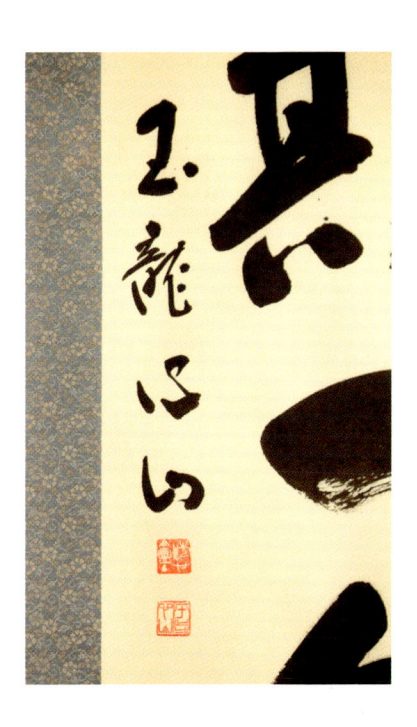

一期一会

"Harmony, respect, purity, tranquility" (*Wa kei sei jaku*)

Hanging scroll, 170x30cm

Commentary by John Stevens

These are the four principles of the tea ceremony.

Commentary by Audrey Seo

This phrase is attributed to the tea master Sen Rikyu (1522-1591) and reflects the essence of the tea ceremony, which has a long association with Zen.

"Harmony" suggests the sense of unity and oneness—with nature, between host and guest, and among the guests at a tea gathering—reflected in the seasonal selection of food and the aesthetic choices of tea wares. This harmony suggests an understanding of the rhythms of the gathering, but also the ability to change accordingly.

"Respect" is demonstrated in the highly ritualised gestures of the tea ceremony—from the interactions with the guests to the handling and appreciation of the utensils. Every refined and precise movement reflects respect.

"Purity" reveals the appreciation for cleanliness, both physical and spiritual. Before a tea gathering, the host meticulously cleans the utensils, and in so doing also purifies his or her mind and heart in preparation. Similarly, as the guests stroll in the garden towards the tea house, they rinse their hands and mouths in stone basins, and pass through small gates. These actions signify the cleansing of one's self and the leaving behind of "dust" from the outside world.

"Tranquility" is achieved when the previous three principles are mastered—the quiet and stillness of jaku is the state in which ideas and thoughts are extinguished.

Shinzan Rōshi uses a basic running style script to write these four characters. The strokes within each character are largely linked from one to the next, creating a fluid dancing quality. Yet each character remains individual and distinct, perhaps reflecting their individual importance as principles in the tea ceremony.

和敬清寂

"A true person of no rank" (*Ichi-mui no shinnin*)

Hanging scroll, 205x80cm

Commentary by John Stevens

Zen master Rinzai's description of the ideal Zen practitioner.

Commentary by Audrey Seo

A monk asked the master Rinzai, "What is the true person of no rank?" Master Rinzai descended from his seat, grabbed the monk, and said, "Speak, speak!" When the monk hesitated, the master released him, and said, "What a shit-stick, this true person of no rank."

Shinzan Rōshi's calligraphy, revealing this rather difficult teaching from the *Rinzai Roku* (Record of Rinzai), is visually striking with its bold, even strokes, its balanced precision and sense of stability and strength. There are no extra flourishes or embellishments, no extraneous motion. It simply is.

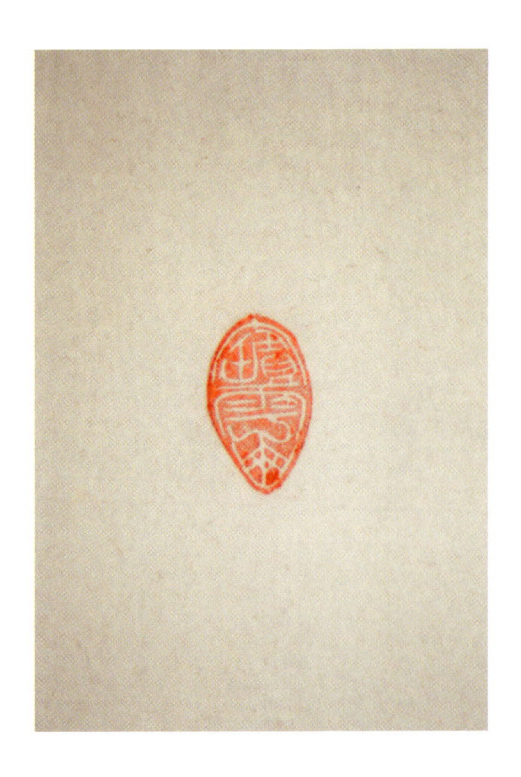

一要位真人

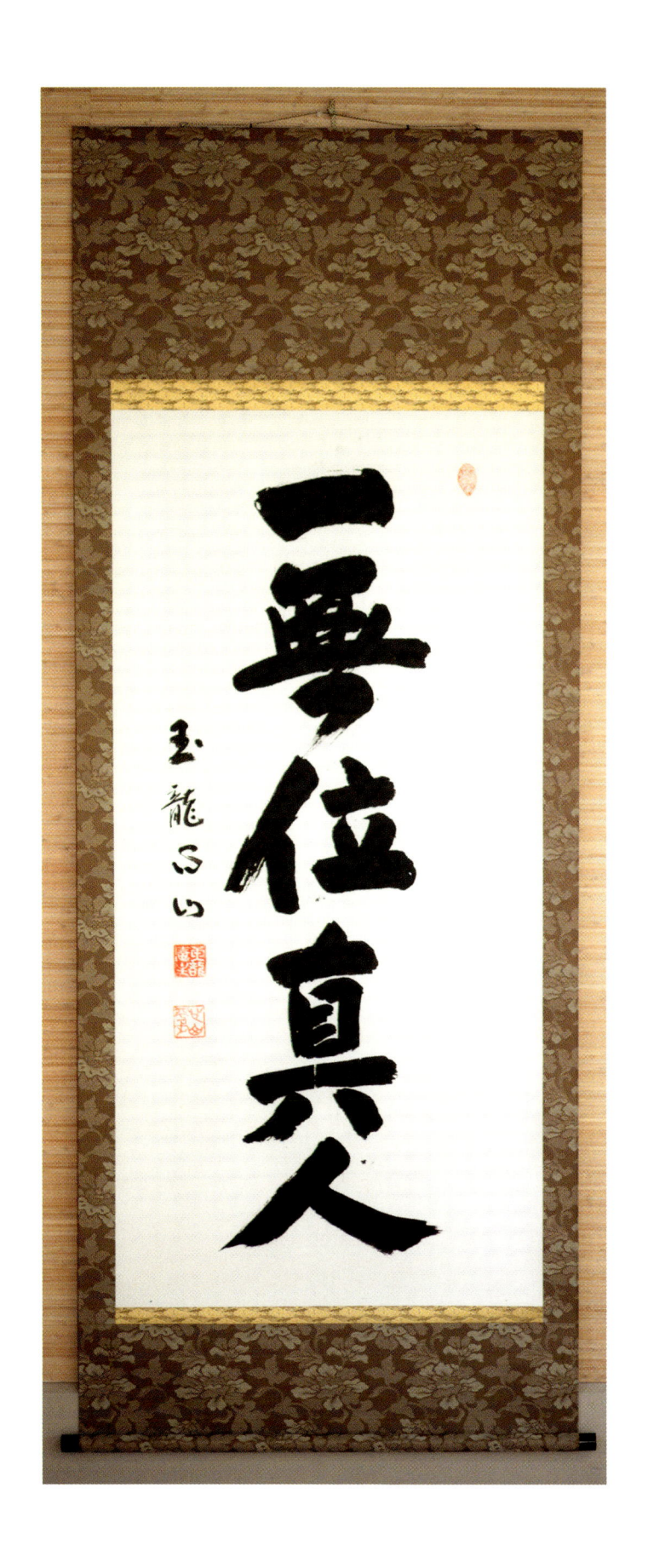

玉龍石山

"The sun rises shining light on heaven and earth"
(*Hi idete kenkon kagayaku*)

Hanging scroll, 165x40cm

Commentary by Audrey Seo

> "When there is light, everything is clearly revealed and nothing is hidden. Worldly illusions are removed and all is good wherever you are."

This is the first part of a two-line verse, the second half of which is,

> "The clouds settle, the mountain peaks are verdant green."

Thus, as enlightenment emerges illusions disappear.

Visually, there are many complex characters here, but Shinzan Rōshi has anchored the work with the first character, "sun" (*hi* 日). This character is developed from the pictograph of a sun which was a simple circle with a dot in the centre. Shinzan Rōshi playfully retains these ancient characteristics in his version.

日出乾坤輝

"No birth or death" (*Mu shoji*)

Card shikishi, 27x24cm

Commentary by Audrey Seo

Birth and death are often considered as dualistic entities fixed within a cycle and dependent upon each other: birth leads to death. But Zen master Dōgen stressed that the two states are not opposing. Instead both are manifestations of a total dynamic process.

Dōgen wrote: "It is a mistake to suppose that birth turns into death. Birth is a phase that is an entire period of itself, with its own past and future. For this reason, in Buddha-dharma, birth is understood as no-birth. Death is a phase that is an entire period of itself, with its own past and future. For this reason, death is understood as no-death." (Trans. by Arnold Kotler and Kazuaki Tanahashi)

輿北生
ふり

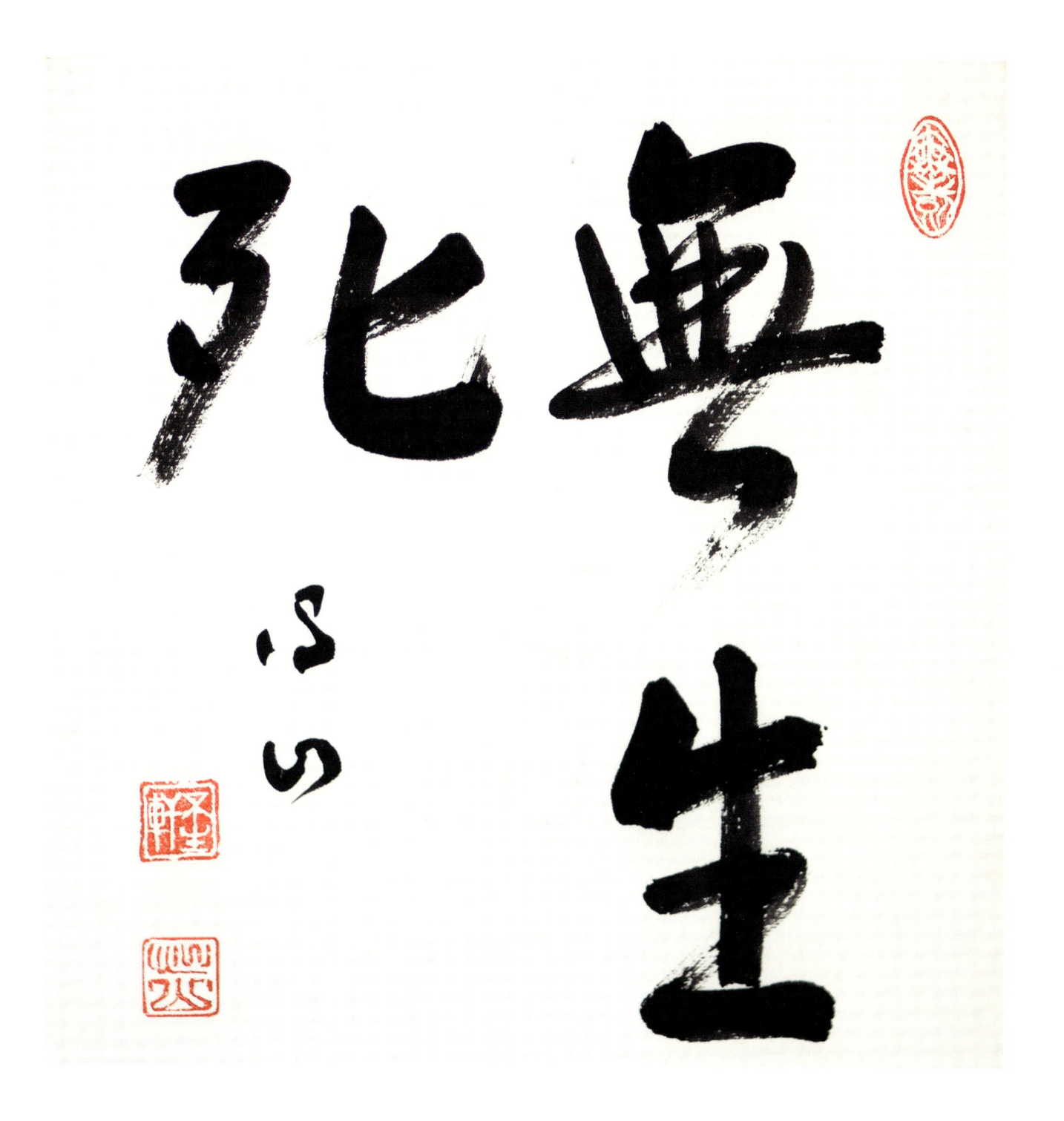

"Yoga practice" (*Yuga-gyo*)

Card shikishi, 32x24cm

Commentary by Audrey Seo

Shinzan Rōshi dynamically brushes the name of the Zenways training hall in London. There is a long tradition of Zen masters writing out the names of important halls and buildings, as well as the spiritual names of the mountains on which the temples are situated. Many of these calligraphies are large in stature and bold in character.

Instead of being mounted into scrolls, they are often framed and hung above doorways. In many cases, the calligraphies are transferred and carved into large wooden boards that can be hung on the outsides of buildings or temple gates. The temples and monasteries of the Obaku sect of Zen are well known for their large carved signboards that designate important structures.

瑜伽行

玉龍心印

Longer Phrases

"Within nothingness there are inexhaustible treasures" (*Mu ichi motsu chu mujinzo*)

Hanging scroll, 205x80cm

Commentary by John Stevens

This is the first part of a two-line phrase:
 Mu ichimotsu chu mujinzo.
 Hana ari tsuki ari rodai ari.

This can be translated as:
 Within nothingness, there are endless treasures.
  There are flowers, and the moon, and pavilions.

Both ancient Buddhist texts and modern quantum physics state that the universe is mostly empty space; yet from that emptiness—an inexhaustible treasure—the universe emerges full of the most wonderful (and concrete) things such as flowers, the moon and pleasure pavilions.

Commentary by Audrey Seo

Applied to Zen practice, when one is able to let go of attachments, self and worldly illusions, then one can fully see and appreciate the beauty of things.

Calligraphically, this is a very interesting work because Shinzan Rōshi has written the two "*mu*" characters next to each other at the top of each column. By comparing them, you can see how differently the same character can be brushed, giving it a different flavour and aesthetic effect. On the right, the character is written in regular/running script, and its structure is still clear and easy to read. In the example at the top of the left column, Shinzan Rōshi has written the character in a much freer, cursive style. These types of variations and manipulations of characters make the reading of calligraphy fascinating and difficult at the same time.

無一物中無尽蔵

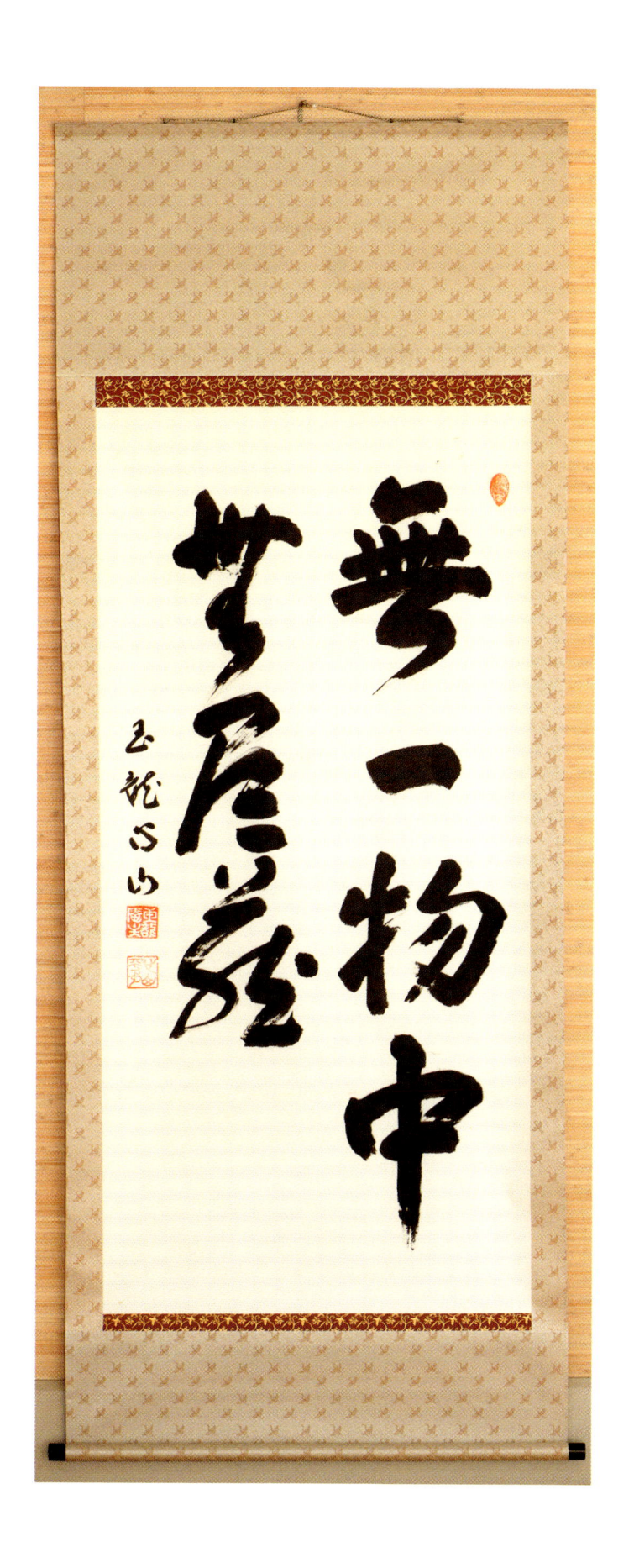

"Spring enters [the] thousand forests — here [and] there, warblers" (*Haru was senrin ni iru shosho uguisu*)

Hanging scroll, 180x44cm

Commentary by John Stevens

Uguisu is a type of Japanese bush warbler. The second half of the verse goes, "In autumn, the moon shines on every home, and reflects upon every body of water." Within the changing of the seasons, Buddha-nature is manifest, and there is no home that is not bathed in the radiance of enlightenment.

Commentary by Audrey Seo

This seven-word poetic line translates word for word: "Spring enters [the] thousand forests — here [and] there, warblers." The sixth character, at the top of the second column, is a repeat sign, forming a compound with the previous character (處) meaning "here and there" or "various places".

This is primarily a literary phrase, but it became popular with Zen masters: on a scroll it would often hang in the *tokonoma* alcove, particularly during springtime tea ceremonies.

Here, the cursive-script calligraphy shows effective contrasts at the beginning of each column. On the right, the initial complex character, "spring" (春) is followed by "enters" (入), made up of only two strokes of the brush; this also forms a kind of visual roof over the "thousand forests" (千林) below it. In reverse, the simple two-dot repeat mark on the left is followed by the complex character "warblers" (鶯), with the smaller signature below. These contrasts, augmented by the actual number of strokes for each character: 4-2-2-3-5-2-7, give the calligraphy its visual rhythm.

This is the first of two phrases, the second line of which is, "Autumn sinks into 10,000 rivers—every home, in moonlight!"

春入千林處々鶯

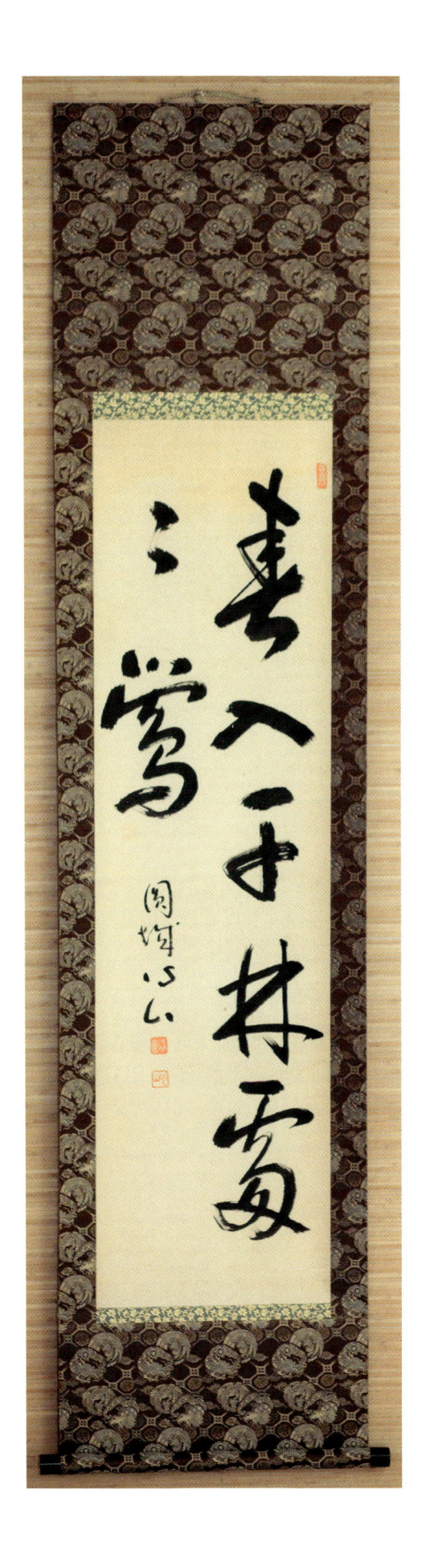

圓爾心人

Zenga – Daruma

Daruma: "Pointing directly to the heart/mind, see your own nature, become Buddha" (*Jikishi ninshin, kensho jobutsu*)

Hanging scroll, 175x45cm

Commentary by John Stevens

In Zen art, the master does not paint Daruma (Bodhidharma, the first patriarch of Zen) as a historical figure but as a symbol of penetrating insight, self-reliance, ceaseless diligence, and the rejection of externals. Thus, a Daruma painting is a spiritual self-portrait, based on the individual experience of each Zen master. When asked, "How long does it take to paint a Daruma?" the great Zen master Hakuin replied, "Ten minutes and eighty years."

Commentary by Audrey Seo

We often see the phrase, "See your own nature, become Buddha," but here we have the full verse attributed to Daruma. To see one's own nature, one must look into one's heart/mind. In western thought the heart is usually associated with emotion, while the mind is considered logical and intellectual, thus they seemingly represent two opposing ideals. But in the Far East, the character 心 (Chinese: "*shin*", Japanese: "*kokoro*") means both heart and mind, so spirit and mind are unified.

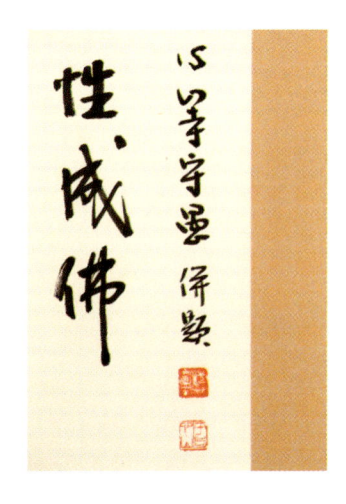

見性成佛
直指人心

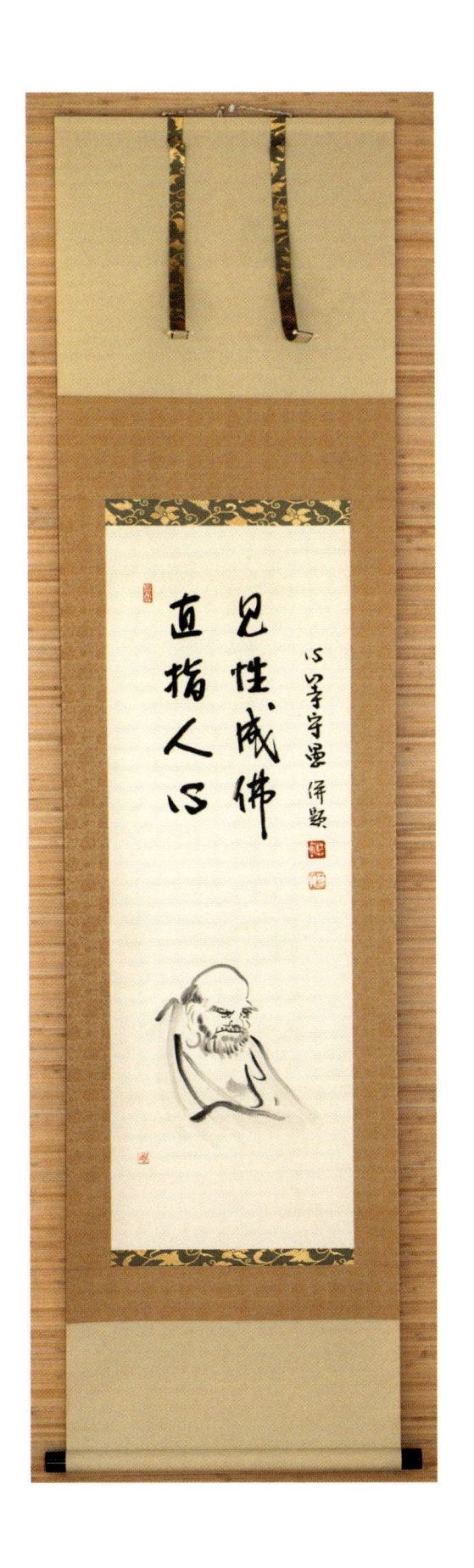

Daruma: "Don't know" (*Fushiki*)

Hanging scroll, 120x45cm

Commentary by Audrey Seo

In this image, the first patriarch of Zen, Daruma, sits with a somewhat worried expression, accented by beautiful ink tones. Above, Shinzan Rōshi has written only two words, "*fushiki*" ("not know", or "don't know")—a reference to the story of Daruma's (Bodhidharma's) meeting with the Chinese Liang Dynasty Emperor Wu in the year 520.

> During their encounter, the emperor asked Daruma what merit was gained from endowing temples and monasteries, to which he answered, "No merit".
> The emperor then enquired about the basic principle of Zen doctrine.
> Daruma replied, "Vast emptiness, nothing sacred."
> "Who then now stands before me?" asked the emperor.
> Daruma replied, "*Fushiki*" (usually translated as "I don't know," but literally meaning, "not know"). This phrase is a *kōan*, as it does not permit an intellectual answer. Who is it who knows, or is known?

Daruma is depicted here as a seated figure with no visible legs. This tradition, now mostly associated with roly-poly Daruma dolls, is a reference to the nine years in which he sat in meditation in front of a wall at a Shaolin temple in the north of China after leaving Emperor Wu's court. During this period of extreme meditation, Daruma's legs are supposed to have fallen off.

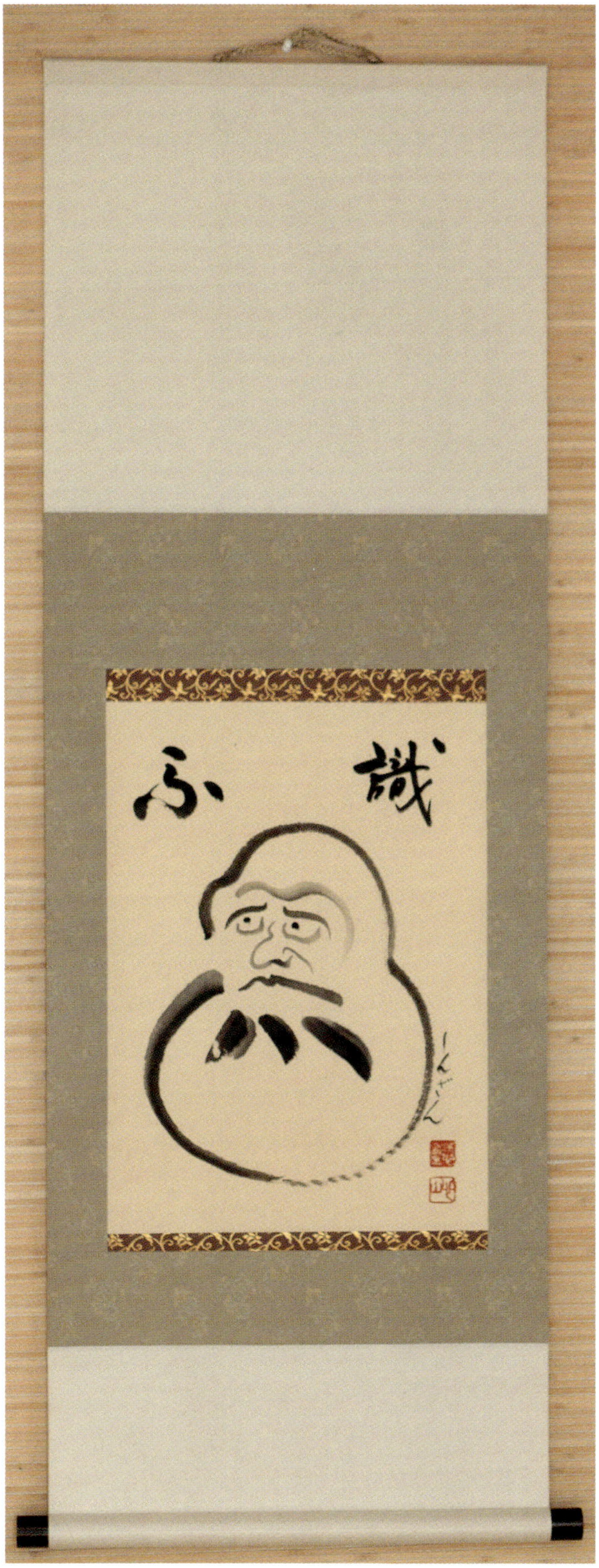

Daruma: "Seven times down, eight times up" (*Nana korobi ya oki*)

Hanging scroll, 180x53cm

Commentary by John Stevens

This is the battle cry of Zen students. This figure is male but sometimes Daruma is portrayed as a lady in Zenga (Zen art), and there are also paintings of "Mr and Mrs. Daruma."

Commentary by Audrey Seo

Here Shinzan Rōshi has brushed a simplified seated Daruma figure from a single curvilinear outline accented by a few quick brushstrokes. This charming figure reflects a gentle, serene expression, eyes downcast and shaded by lovely bushy grey brows. In this case, the image of a legless, roly-poly seated figure reveals cultural connotations. The phrase, "seven times down, eight times up" ("*nana korobi ya oki*") is a traditional Japanese expression that reflects the Japanese social ideal of resilience. When you face hardship or get knocked down, you get up again, no matter how many times you must try. This sense of perseverance and determination is found in all aspects of Japanese culture, and has been apparent even under the most horrendous conditions, including the 2011 tsunami in Fukushima.

The image of round-bottomed Daruma figures was transformed into *okiagari koboshi* ("tumbler dolls"), which became popular during a smallpox epidemic during the Edo period (1600-1868). When knocked down, the dolls pop back up, thereby representing a quick recovery from illness, the encouragement to persevere under the harshest conditions, and the determination and resilience to maintain one's Zen practice.

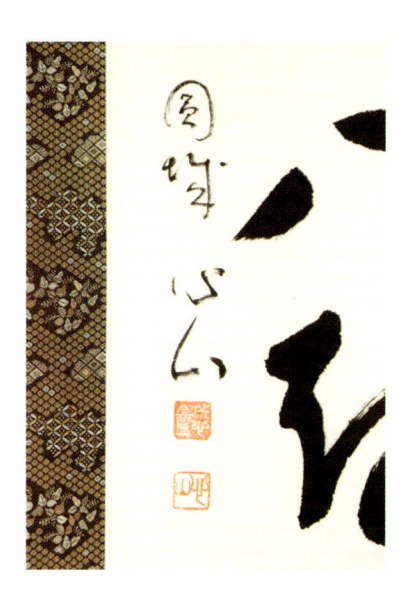

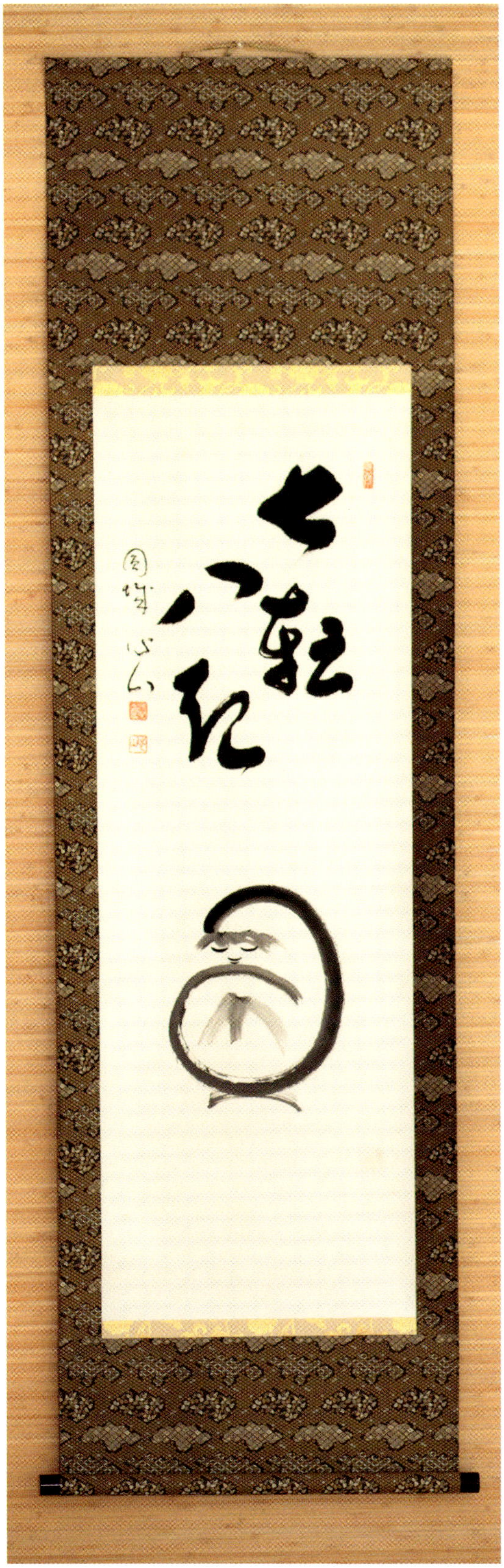
七転八起

Zenga – Kannon

Kannon: "An unlimited ocean of good fortune and longevity" (*Fukuju kai mu ryo*)

Hanging scroll, 115x55cm

Commentary by John Stevens

In Zen art, depictions of Kannon—the queen of compassion who strives to save sentient beings through her unlimited use of skilful means—are equally as important as portraits of Daruma. While Daruma represents the hard-edged, intense, internal dimension of Zen practice, Kannon symbolises the softer, embracing, external dimension. Both aspects—insight and compassion—are essential for complete understanding of the Zen experience. That is why a good Zen master can identify with both the masculine and feminine elements in his or her Buddha-nature and create inspired paintings of either a gruff Daruma or a lovely Kannon.

Commentary by Audrey Seo

Here we see the Bodhisattva Kannon seated with an incense burner, gazing over a sutra book. The inscription is a reference to a couplet from the *Kannon Sutra*, which forms chapter 25 of the *Lotus Sutra*,

> "Regarding with compassionate eyes all sentient beings
> And accumulating good fortune like an ocean without limit."

The rich ink and confident fluidity of the inscription to the left provide a visual balance to the grey tones and dreamy nature of the figure.

Referred to as a "white-robed Kannon", the figure bears a beautifully serene facial expression, having taken on a very feminine appearance, as is common in east Asian depictions, despite starting out as a male figure in India.

The large halo can also be seen as the moon—perhaps the bodhisattva is reciting from the *Kannon Sutra*, or perhaps he is simply basking in the radiant purity of the moonlight.

The Zen master Hakuin wrote,

> "Enlightened beings of higher faculties always sit and recline in the variety of different situations in action; you see everything before your eyes as your own original true clean face, just as if your were looking at your face in a mirror."
>
> (Thomas Cleary, trans., Kensho: *The Heart of Zen*. Boston: Shambhala, 1997, pp73-74).

福壽海無量

Kannon: "The pure wisdom light (of Kannon) breaks through the darkness (of ignorance)"
(*Fu ku sho jo ko, e nichi ha sho an*)

Hanging scroll, 185x45cm

Commentary by Audrey Seo

Kannon is probably the most popular bodhisattva in the Buddhist pantheon, reflecting great compassion for all. In Zen images, Kannon is typically depicted seated in a serene and relaxed manner on a small island, which is iconographically derived from the bodhisattva's traditional home, Mount Potalaka. Often dressed in a white robe, this Kannon is also often referred to as the "Water Moon Kannon" because of the traditional setting of lapping waves and a halo moon in the background. In Zen, Kannon represents assistance and encouragement for those seeking enlightenment.

The inscription is taken from Chapter 25 of the famous *Lotus Sutra (Hokke Kyo)*, extolling the salvific power of compassion.

恵日破諸闇
無垢清浄光

Fu ku sho jo ko
E nichi ha sho an

The pure wisdom light (of Kannon)
Breaks through the darkness (of ignorance)

惠日破諸闇
無垢清淨光

Zenga – other

Dragon staff: "A leisurely stroll under the blue sky" (*Senten heiho*)

Hanging scroll, 190x60cm

Commentary by Audrey Seo

Images of dragon staffs are generally associated with the transmission of the dharma from master to disciple. The imagery of the "dragon staff" is derived from case number 60 in the *Hekiganroku*, "Ummon's Staff Becomes a Dragon", in which the T'ang Dynasty Zen master Ummon (Ch. Yun-men, died 949) says: "My staff has transformed itself into a dragon and swallowed the universe! Where are the mountains, the rivers, and the great world?" The dragon thus becomes a symbol for the student who has successfully experienced enlightenment.

The white horse hair whisk is also a symbol of the Zen abbot and his teaching being transmitted from master to student.

These images are most notably associated with the Zen master Hakuin (1685-1768), who developed the visual theme over time, beginning with standard depictions of a thin gnarled staff encircled by the master's flywhisk. In subsequent examples, the top of the staff gradually developed a hole, but it still retained the appearance of a wooden staff. Then slowly the top of the staff began to bend slightly and the hole widened until, by the late 1750s, the top of the staff had transformed into a dragon's head, complete with a large eye socket and a mouth grasping the whisk.

Over time, later examples included a pupil to the eye socket and a more pronounced dragon's muzzle, until eventually the image appeared to be more dragon than staff. Ironically, lest his followers take the image too literally, Hakuin commented on the *kōan* from the *Hekiganroku*, stating,

> "There is no such thing as turning into a dragon. From the perspective of the staff directly swallowing the universe, there's no need to turn into a dragon and grab the clouds and fog to fly; even those who have passed through the three tiers of locks are not live dragons."
> Thomas Cleary, trans., *Secrets of Blue Cliff Record*. Shambhala, 2000, p205

青天平歩

心山筆

"Longevity" (*Ennen*) with pine

Hanging scroll, 110x66cm

Commentary by Daizan Rōshi

The first kanji "*en*" means to extend, prolong, "*nen*" means year, so the two together, *ennen*, mean "longevity".

The evergreen nature of the pine together with its endurance have made it a symbol of longevity. Chapter 16 of the *Lotus Sutra* reveals that the Buddha's lifespan is essentially beginningless and endless. In Zen practice we come to realise our place in this beginningless, endless life—we find our true longevity.

延年

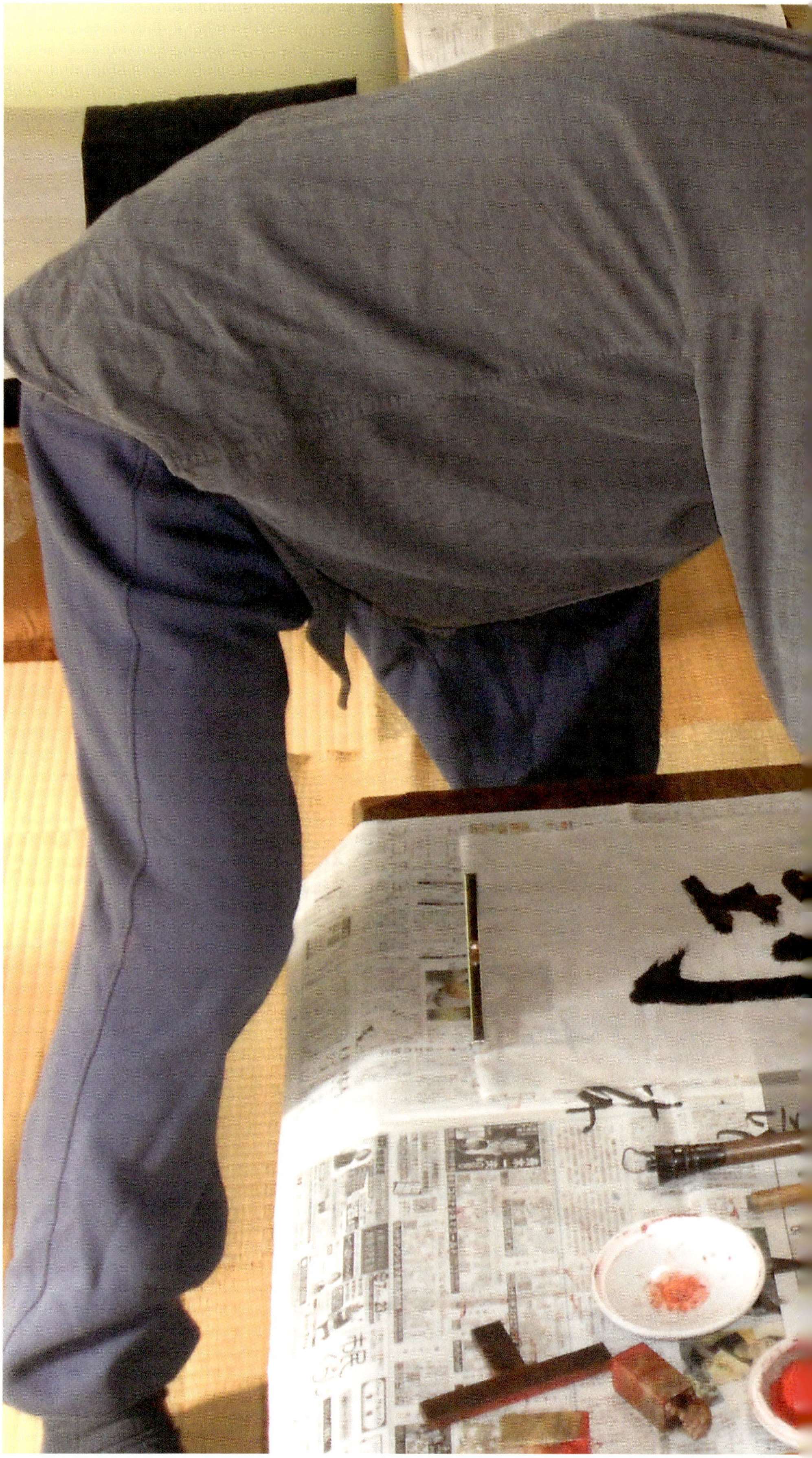

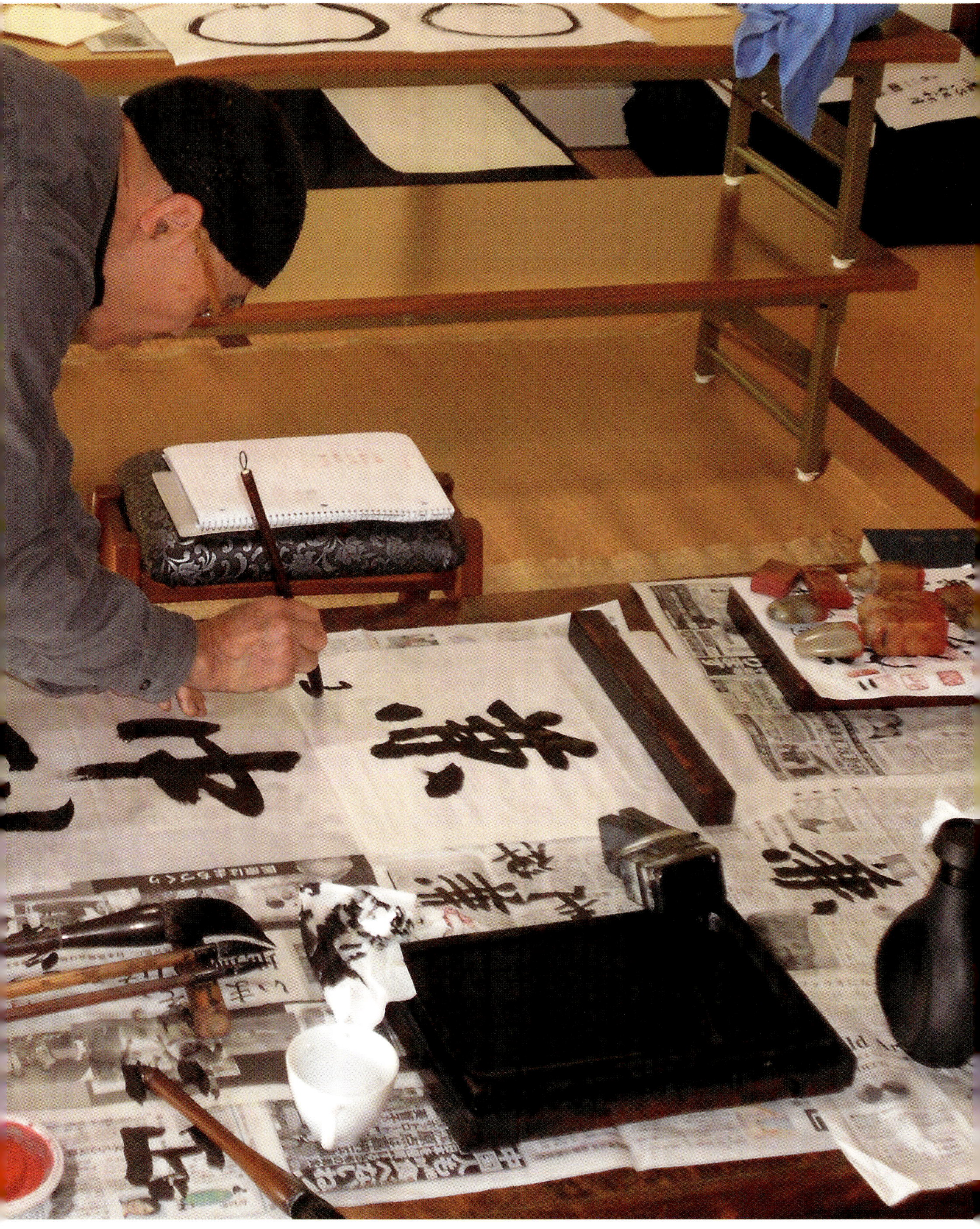

Appreciating Zen Art: An Interview with Audrey Yoshiko Seo, Zen Scholar

Dr. Seo has spent a quarter of a century introducing Westerners to the mysteries of Zen art. She is well acquainted with what is needed to help us truly see these works and has published a number of influential books on the subject. In reflecting on Shinzan Rōshi's work, she comments, "There is a sense of openness and a willingness and desire to go beyond tradition, to step outside the box and reach people, much like [Zen master] Hakuin."

How did you get interested in Zen art?

As an undergraduate studying history at Brandeis University (Boston, Massachusetts), I took a class on Chinese art. About halfway through the semester we got to Ch'an painting and my professor showed Muchi's "Six Persimmons;" I was amazed, I had never seen anything like or imagined there was anything like it. After a few more art history classes, I decided to go to graduate school in art history. I ended up at the University of Kansas, and astonishingly, during my second semester there, the Spencer Museum on campus exhibited "The Art of Zen: Paintings and Calligraphies by Japanese Monks: 1600-1925," curated by Stephen Addiss, who was a professor at the university. Somehow, it was fate. I took the graduate seminar that was offered in conjunction with the show, which continued to open my eyes and mind to Zen. But most importantly, having the actual works by Hakuin, Sengai, Torei, Fugai etc. literally upstairs from the seminar room to see up close for weeks on end was invaluable. You have to see the art. The museum had a huge number of public programmes coinciding with the exhibition, one of which was an artist in residence, who in this case was a Zen master, Fukushima Keido of Tofuku-ji in Kyoto. He gave public calligraphy demonstrations and Zen lectures, which further influenced my interest in Zen art. I eventually wrote my dissertation on Hakuin, and, largely due to my friendship with Fukushima Rōshi, eventually curated and co-wrote "The Art of Twentieth-Century Zen."

Who is your favourite Zen artist and why?

I have spent a lot of time working on Hakuin, writing a dissertation on his work, and also co-curating an exhibition of his work and co-authoring the accompanying catalogue. Hakuin's teachings, writing, and artwork are unsurpassed. He reached an enormous audience with his art, which reveals an amazing amount of variety, creativity and cultural/social exploration. Hakuin made contributions to Zen teaching and art that no one had done before or has done since.

Having said that, I have to say that my favorite Zen artist is Torei Enji, Hakuin's dharma heir. Torei was an extremely serious and earnest Zen practitioner, his writings, while not as numerous as Hakuin's, are also extremely important. But what I like about Torei's art is that it is simply what it is. Most people would consider it a mess (see example shown on facing page). He brushed his characters with wild abandon, creating bold, completely untrammelled works that hit you right in the face. The viewer is not left to ponder aesthetics, composition, balance, or grace. It is immediate and direct, almost as if he didn't give a damn. Torei was in the moment. His work shows that Zen calligraphy is unique—it doesn't have to be "skilled," precise, or technically perfect. Zen calligraphy goes beyond traditional calligraphic ideals—it is an expression of the Zen mind and experience. Torei's work is an expression of this.

How is the artist's character expressed?

Generally, I believe the artist's character is expressed through the brushwork. The Chinese have long believed that one's nature is revealed through the brush because it reflects the motion and energy from your hand, through your arm, and ultimately through your whole body and mind. You don't hold a brush the way you hold a pencil with your wrist resting on the table; calligraphy requires the entire body to be involved. In Zen, the artist's character is also expressed through their choice of phrases or images. Some phrases are popular Zen phrases that many Zen masters choose to write because they are familiar, but I think many Zen masters also have a few phrases that they have some personal connection to, that resonate with them in particular, or that they believe are most useful in their teaching of Zen.

Some Zen masters, such as Shinzan Rōshi, also paint images. This reveals a desire to go beyond written teachings to approachable imagery. Many Zen masters paint portraits of Daruma (see calligraphy on p110), and each master brings their own spirit and Zen mind to the image. Comparing Daruma images by different Zen masters can be quite telling. And in the case of masters such as Hakuin or Sengai, who did a wide variety of images, you sense that their personalities naturally looked outward at everything and everyone in the world around them. They truly captured the essence of Zen in everyday moments and activities, and also saw and used humour with great effect.

What do you see when you look at Shinzan Rōshi's calligraphies?

Looking at Shinzan Rōshi's calligraphy, I see an artist and Zen master who likes variety, who does not want to be limited to one style or even to standard Zen phrases. He does not even want to be limited by language, writing in English as well as Chinese and Japanese. Some of his works reveal bold, structured characters reflecting strength and directness, while other works demonstrate a more fluid, cursive style, which allows the characters to dance and float down the composition. There is a sense of openness and a willingness and desire to go beyond tradition, to step outside the box and reach people, much like Hakuin. Shinzan Rōshi also occasionally experiments with painting which adds to his calligraphic work, making it more approachable.

"Three Shinto Deities" by Torei Enji (ink on paper, 130x53cm) (reproduced with permission from Dr. Seo)

Many Zen students (Eastern and Western) feel daunted by this art form. What do they stand to gain by becoming familiar with it?

I think people are becoming less and less daunted by calligraphy. Having taught undergraduates, off and on, for 25 years I have seen them become much more comfortable with the art form. Students today in many ways don't think twice about it, it is not "foreign," it has become a part of their own visual world, even if they can't "read" it. They see it as movement, energy, expression, structure, shape and even words, that they do not necessarily need to understand in order to appreciate. Some students are probably more comfortable with and more able to appreciate calligraphy than a Renaissance painting.

Becoming more and more familiar with Zen calligraphy in particular allows people to better understand the Zen mind. I believe that brushwork by Zen masters resonates with a particular energy or spirit that is a reflection of their Zen mind. This probably sounds like holistic mumbo jumbo, but I think brushwork by Zen masters is special. It is spiritual/religious artwork done by the religious teachers themselves. These are not works of religious imagery commissioned by religious leaders to be done by professional artists. Zen art is the direct expression of each Zen master's own experiences from training, through enlightenment, and ultimately as a teacher. Every encounter, every experience, every moment is captured. As a result, because it is not done by professional artists, Zen brushwork is not always "pretty," but it is authentic and a true expression of years of training and also of the specific moment it is created. Becoming more and more familiar with Zen calligraphy will, hopefully, enable people to see and feel this.

How is it if you build a relationship with a calligraphy, living with it over a period of time?

Sometimes, when you hang a work of art on the wall, you are excited about it and look at it with appreciation for a while, and then over time it starts to blend into the environment and you take less and less notice of it. Good calligraphy, especially Zen calligraphy does not allow this to happen. Calligraphy, even if it is not big and bold, has a subtly and sublime elegance that always catches your eye, perhaps because of its very nature as a gestural action. A painting is an image that represents a whole, even though you can and should always look at small aspects of it. But when you look at a painting, you have no idea where the artist started and stopped. You cannot see the process. Calligraphy is like a musical score, if you can read music, you can read the notes and notations—you know the sounds, the rhythm, the speed. You can "read" calligraphy the same way. Because calligraphy is generally written in columns and because there are rules on how each character is written (order of strokes), you know where the artist started the calligraphy, and you can follow each gesture through the entire work. You don't have to be able to read the words to understand the energy, the feeling, even the process of where the artists stopped to re-dip the brush in ink, how certain characters might be emphasised by size or dramatic gesture. Is the aesthetic of the brushwork structured and architectural, is it fluid and elegant, or bold and dynamic? By seeing and following the process, the viewer is also actively involved in the gesture themselves. It is not just about looking at an image or a word, it is about the process: everything from the Zen master's experience to the moment the brush moved across the paper that the viewer is absorbing. I believe it is a much more active, involved form of seeing than with other types of art.

Living with calligraphy over time allows you to become aware of these things because the artwork almost demands it. You always see new things in a calligraphy, no matter how many times you look at it. Zen calligraphy in particular brings all these aspects as well as a depth and richness of spirit to the viewer.

Our western students typically don't read kanji (Japanese characters). How much do they lose in appreciating this art?

It is always best to have a translation of the kanji so as to understand the words and gain the full value of the teaching, or poetry etc. However, in terms of appreciating calligraphy as art, you do not have to be able to read kanji. Again, people who have grown up in the post-abstract expressionist world understand gesture. What if we suddenly learned that there are hidden "words" in Franz Kline's paintings? Does that mean that all of our appreciation of his works as abstractions up to now have been meaningless? Of course not. If I do not know Christian iconography, does this mean I cannot appreciate a beautiful medieval painting? Beautiful, powerful gestures of the brush can be appreciated as form, as movement, and again in the case of Zen calligraphy, knowing that the Zen master is expressing his enlightened mind enhances the work beyond words. Some connoisseurs of calligraphy often find the ability to read the words a distraction from being able to purely enjoy and appreciate the calligraphy for its own merits, to just see the dance.

How would you guide a beginner in finding their way into this art form?

Just start looking. Eventually, you will start seeing. Do not have expectations of having immediate epiphanies about Zen, about life or anything else. Just look. Follow the brush, look at the composition, consider the negative as well as the positive space. Look at balance— how each individual character is balanced like a form of architecture, and also how the totality of the composition is balanced. Does strong, angular calligraphy make you react differently than fluid, cursive calligraphy? Why? You may decide that you like certain types or styles of calligraphy better than others. This is great because it means you are developing your eye and making aesthetic distinctions and valuations. But always try to articulate why you are making these judgements.

Gradually, if you study enough pieces with their translations, you will soon be able to pick out certain characters— in other words, you will have learned to "read" without realising it. And remember, many characters are derived from pictographs, so they are easy to identify, "mountain" for instance (山) looks like a mountain, or "moon" (月), originally a pictograph of a quarter moon, and of course you often see the word "shin" (心 heart/mind) in Zen calligraphy. If you spend enough time looking and comparing, you will eventually be able to read certain common characters not only in clearly delineated block script, but also in more cursive scripts.

ZEN MASTER SHINZAN – A LIFE IN FIVE CALLIGRAPHIES

© 大浩
月 BAERNDAL

135

Founder of the Japanese tea ceremony, Sen no Rikyu (1522-1591 CE) once said, "A calligraphy in which the words of the Buddha or ancestors and the virtue of the calligrapher function together makes for the finest of scrolls and a notable treasure."

Other sections in this book discuss the art-historical and cultural aspects of Zen master Shinzan's works. This section covers the eventful half a century of Zen practice that has formed this particular "Zen character". His story is told around five of his calligraphies, highlighting different aspects of his life and teachings.

Purification Of The Heart

In Japan, a newborn baby is counted as one year old. So, in accordance with this Japanese reckoning, Shinzan Rōshi's students celebrated his 80th birthday at Gyokuryuji on 2nd July 2014. According to Western counting this birthday is a year later.

Most of the works on show for his London art exhibition have been created specifically for the event, between these two birthdays, during his 80th year. The scroll pictured here, "Sen Shin" (Purify the Heart/Mind; described in detail on p70) is an example of Shinzan Rōshi's most mature work.

There are many threads represented by this particular piece, some of which I suspect you may recognise in your own life. This was what he told me of how the events of his life unfolded.

Junichi Miyamae (later given the ordained name Shinzan) was born in northern Japan on the banks of a great river called Agano Gawa. His father was a hydro-electric engineer. When war against the Allies started, the boy was five years old. Towards the end of the wartime period life was very hard in Japan. There was constant bombing, a lot of hunger and an awful lot of worries about what was going to happen, as the Americans were gradually moving up through the Japanese islands. Shinzan told me how, in his area, the school system gradually broke down. Instead of going to school, he joined a group of nine- and 10-year-old boys who were placed under the supervision of a 14-year-old. Each boy had a sharpened bamboo stick. They spent their days rehearsing killing Americans with these makeshift spears—everyone expected guerrilla war. Shinzan felt certain he would die, and it was his duty to try to take at least one enemy with him.

There was a very clear sense of the primitive bamboo sticks against American firepower. Practising like this, day after day after day, had a powerful effect on the young Shinzan. And then suddenly the atomic bombs were dropped and the war was over. The next thing he knew, there was an American soldier in the village who was very friendly, giving the kids sweets and teaching them how to play baseball. Something completely unwound in Shinzan and I remember, as he told this story to me, he simply said: "I cried." He went from viewing the Americans and all foreigners as the enemy, to realising that things were not like that at all. Ever since that time he has always been particularly open to westerners—unlike many Zen teachers. So in some ways we have that anonymous American soldier to thank for us being able to practise Zen today.

As a young man growing up in the post-war period, life was poor. The country was pretty much burned to the ground, there was a lot of hunger and insecurity. The first priority was to try to look after basic material needs. At university in Kyoto, Shinzan studied business. He had great plans to become a successful businessman, make plenty of money for himself and for his family, and also to provide for others and build the general economic wellbeing of the country.

In his boyhood, Shinzan had come across Buddhism only tangentially. Occasionally a Buddhist priest would come to the house and chant at the family altar for a few minutes. His mother would give the priest some money and off he would go. That was Shinzan's sole exposure to Buddhism and he was unimpressed. To this day he is vehement in stating his belief that the whole business of chanting for money is a useless process.

After graduation Shinzan went into business. He began working for a big construction corporation, before going on to found his own company delivering building materials and products. He was a very poor negotiator and gave customers excessively good deals, which ate into his profit margins. Consequently his little company was under a lot of financial pressure.

There was a typhoon one night. The company had an urgent delivery to make but the lorry driver was fearful of the weather and refused to go. So our young business hero pulled the driver out of the way, climbed into the cab of the lorry, drove off into the night and the storm, was involved in an accident and someone died. Of course, this was a huge disaster for all concerned. Quite soon the company folded.

He then got involved in another business venture. In post-war Japan cooking oil was very much at a premium and he began trading it, supplying it to restaurants and other institutions. At this point he not only put all his remaining funds into this enterprise but pretty much all of his parents' money as well.

He was no more successful in the cooking oil business than he was in construction supplies. He managed to lose not only his own money, but his parents' investment as well, and felt an utter failure.

At this point he was so disgusted with himself that he felt the only course of action was suicide. He went down to the railway, put his head on the tracks and waited for a train. But he just could not go through with it. Being unable even to kill himself compounded his feeling of failure.

One day, by chance, he was driving past a railway station. A Buddhist nun from the Rinzai Zen school was waiting in the rain for a taxi. There were not many taxis in post-war Japan, so sometimes it would be quite a wait. So he pulled up and offered the nun a lift back to her temple. She got in. He was struck by the brightness and warmth of her character.

A few days later he was amazed to find her on his doorstep with a book. It was an old Zen text called *Sen Shin Roku*, "The Record of Purifying the Heart". It took a while for him to begin reading but when he finally did, one sentence hit him right between the eyes: "Zen is beyond life and death." This was what he needed.

He sought out the nun. Now he was overflowing with questions. She would not answer, laughingly calling herself a foolish old woman. But reading the book and meeting this living exemplar of what it was about gave the young man a new sense of possibility. He had felt an utter failure. Now he saw a chance to find a basis that would bring value, meaning and purpose. The nun recognised the shift and took him to her teacher, Mitsui Daishin, a Zen master in Gifu, a city in central Japan. And the young man in quite short order decided that he was going to throw his life into an earnest search for the truth of things. Nothing else had worked out for him, so this was what he was going to do.

The nuns in their little temple were quite taken with this earnest young man and supported him in his quest. They made his robes for him and began to prepare him to step into a new world. So quite soon after this he entered the *sōdō*, the training monastery, as an *unsui*—a cloud-water monk, the most junior of the monastic ranks. Like clouds and water, an *unsui* is free and unfixed so that he can commit his all to his spiritual search.

His training temple was called Zuiryoji. It had been restored in 1806 by Zen master Inzan, one of the systematisers of the Zen practice of studying *kōans* or "spiritual questions". In referring to Inzan's dynamic and fearless character, Shinzan Rōshi told me how when studying the *kōan*, "Put out the fire on the other side of the mountain", Inzan entered the *sanzen* room (the private interview room where a trainee expresses his understanding) with a huge bucket of water and poured it right over his teacher.

Although connected with such an illustrious master, Zuiryoji was nevertheless not in the highest rank of Zen training centres. It was sited in central Gifu, a medium-sized city, about the size of Bristol. It was a simple matter to climb over the wall at night and frolic in the town, so the monastery did not really attract the most serious Zen students.

Once the teacher, Daishin Rōshi, recognised the sincerity of this new young monk, he decided to send him off to his own teacher's temple, deep in the mountains, far from distractions and temptations.

It had the reputation of being the strictest training monastery in Japan, and was nicknamed "*Oni Sōdō*" ("Devil's Dōjō"). Its ascetic reputation has roots in the Middle Ages, when Zen monk Kanzan Egen had a deep realisation and disappeared into the mountains to mature it. For eight years he spent his days working as an anonymous cowman and his nights in *zazen* (seated meditation practice) on the edge of a precipice. Eventually the emperor had Kanzan traced and brought to the capital.

The humble Kanzan was a man of few words and taught very simply. Once a monk came to ask him about the matter of birth and death. The master replied, "There is no birth and death around [Kanzan] Egen." It is said that when death approached, Kanzan, dressed in the simple clothes of a travelling monk, stood in front of the temple and died on his feet. Eventually Shōgenji monastery was built on the spot of Kanzan's mountain retreat and this was where Shinzan came to train with Zen master Kajiura Itsugai.

Itsugai was stout and fierce. In his lectures, he often urged on his monks with stories of his own practice. As an *unsui* at Kyoto's Daitokuji monastery, every single one of his contemporaries had experienced the joyful awakening of *kenshō*—the perception of one's own true nature. Itsugai alone had not found this. He vowed to meditate all night in the temple graveyard for 100 days. It was in the middle of winter and of all Japan, Kyoto is notable for its winter cold. Even when snow fell on him, the earnest young monk did not falter in his practice. When he went to see his teacher for morning *sanzen*, sometimes Itsugai would faint from cold. He battled on through the hundred days, seeming to make no progress at all.

Then came a rest day. The Daitokuji monks wandered into the city, but not Itsugai. He spent a little time at a nearby shrine his mother used to visit. He bowed his head and prayed that his spiritual eye would open. Then he returned to Daitokuji and continued his meditation. Evening came. It began to get dark, but the monks had not yet returned. Their laundry was still hanging outside, so he brought it in, mindfully folded it and placed it in front of their rooms. In a Zen monastery, the rest day is also the bathing day, so Itsugai prepared the bath. He filled the furnace with firewood. Unconsciously, automatically he piled on more wood and lit the fire. All of a sudden a stream of fire and heat came out and hit his body. At that moment he realised his true nature. The returning monks found him dancing and singing with joy.

Scans of photos that perished in the fire at Gyokuryuji in 2005.
Top-left: the young Junichi as a schoolboy; bottom-left: a family portrait of the Miyamae family—the young Junichi with his two sisters and brother and his parents; top centre: Junichi as a teenager; centre: two photos of him with his mother; bottom second-from-right: Junichi the business man; top-right: Shinzan Rōshi doing waterfall practice in Kyūshū; bottom-right: Shinzan with his teacher, Itsugai Rōshi.

Initially Itsugai Rōshi would not even allow the new young monk to come to *sanzen* interviews to formally begin his practice. Basically, he said: "Until you've done what I did, until you've had *kenshō*, you're on your own." Why would he do this?

Well, Itsugai Rōshi was quite old fashioned. As many people have noted, there are really two types of Zen in Japan now. Some people in the Zen world are essentially rather like the priest who came to Shinzan Rōshi's house when he was a boy. Their main business is funerals—and I use the term "business" advisedly. In Japan funerals have become very expensive. It could cost between US$5,000 and US$6,000 to have a funeral and they are nearly always conducted through a Buddhist temple. So some people in the Zen world, in the Japanese Buddhist world, are in the business of making quite a lot of money doing funerals. There are historical reasons for how this situation has arisen.

When there is a lot of money involved in any situation, it can tip the balance of power in a negative direction. It is important to stress, however, that there are many Zen people whose primary motivation is not money. Some, like Shinzan Rōshi, end up outside the large institutional structures; others do their best within the system.

Recently a number of Zen people have indicated to me their wish to go beyond commercialism to the Buddha's original instruction to his followers that they live like bees taking just a little nectar from each flower, thus harming none.

There is an old *kōan*, or Zen case that we study, that contains the line: "Dragons and snakes co-mingle." We could say this describes the condition of the Zen monasteries. Most trainees are just there for a relatively short time, perhaps a year or two. They are sent by their families to do a kind of boot-camp training period so that they can then be authorised to go off to the villages and start to make money doing funerals. Mixed in are Zen students who are not interested in the funeral business but seek spiritual development.

Itsugai Rōshi, this very severe Zen teacher, would not see people for interview until they demonstrated that they were serious. Shinzan went off and spent a week practising meditation by himself in a cave. He did not actually find what he sought, but when he was walking back to the temple it just so happened that Itsugai Rōshi was driving past. The Zen master noticed the young monk, stopped, wound his window down and asked: "What are you doing?" When Shinzan explained to him where he had come from, his sincerity was recognised and Itsugai Rōshi started to teach him.

Shinzan practised very hard. *Sōdō* life was extremely demanding. The hierarchy was rigid. Junior monks had to obey instantly and without question. As well as the hours of *zazen* punctuated by blows from the *keisaku* (the awakening stick), each day contained mindful physical work, largely in the mountains. Roughly once a week the monks put on straw sandals and went through the villages on *takuhatsu* (alms round). Because the temple was remote and distances long, they usually ran. It was normal to return to Shōgenji at the end of the day with bleeding feet. Shinzan happened to be very skilled in massage and often Itsugai Rōshi would call for his aid. Once, at the end of a *takuhatsu* day, Shinzan was called in to give a massage but he was so exhausted that he literally fell asleep in the middle of it. Unusually, the fierce Zen master let him sleep and Shinzan woke up in the middle of the night lying on Itsugai's legs!

Not only was the life simple, it was very unintellectual. The Shōgenji Zen masters were known as the "lineage of fools" (*gudon no keifu*). The approach is summed up in an incident in 1872 when the government launched a general persecution of Buddhism. Every Buddhist priest and nun in the nation was required to take a qualifying examination for the position of doctrinal instructor. The doctrines they were required to teach included revering the emperor and the government. Those who failed were to be expelled from the clergy. Those who passed were graded into ranks.

Shōgenji's Zen master, Tairyu, a deeply spiritual man was summoned to Tokyo for examination. He travelled with his attendant, Seishu, who was brilliant.
In the examination, Tairyu simply responded to each question, "I don't know."
The examiner, exasperated, exclaimed, "If you can't answer these questions, how can you possibly be a teacher?"
Tairyu shouted back, "I don't know." The examiner slammed his fist on the desk. Tairyu simply sat there peacefully.

It was only through the intervention of a high-ranking Zen priest that Tairyu was allowed back to Shōgenji with the lowest possible grade of instructor. His attendant, however, was awarded the rank *dai kogi*—senior lecturer. The government scheme was thus subverted and eventually abandoned.

In later years Seishu would say of the training with Zen master Tairyu: "I used to be intelligent but under his guidance I became a fool." Itsugai constantly exhorted his young charge to do the same—but there was another element in the mix. Shinzan's *unsui* name was a reminder of this central teaching: "*Shugu*"—*Shu* meaning "keep or maintain" and *gu* means "fool or stupid". Day to day he was addressed as *Gu-san* or "Reverend Stupid". But he couldn't simply rest in the unthinking ritual of temple life. Itsugai Rōshi, believing that the post-war world required an emphasis on education, had founded Shōgen Junior College on the edge of the temple grounds. Shinzan was sent there for academic Buddhist studies. At the end of each study day, he had to drop off all he had learned and throw himself wholeheartedly back into the *sōdō* training. The flexibility of mind he acquired remains with him to the present day. Eventually he was required to combine *sōdō* life with teaching at the college.

The inner basis of the *sōdō* training was the *kōans* of the Mino branch of the Inzan line. Many people are aware of the question, "You know the clapping sound made by two hands, but what is the sound of one hand?" Less well known is the fact that there are hundreds of others. Even around this "one hand" question there are many associated ones such as:
"How do you use this one hand in daily life?"
"What is the source of the one hand?"
"When your body turns to dust and ashes, where will the one hand go?"

Monks were expected to focus on each *kōan* in turn in meditation to the point where the monk and the *kōan* became one. The *kōans* were arranged in series to provide a full curriculum of development. Early *kōans* emphasise non-dual or non-separate awareness; later ones explore bringing this awareness into practical life and even, eventually, over-arching systems of Zen theory. To become a Zen master, Shinzan was expected to pass all of them.

The food was thin and simple. The staple was rice mixed with barley combined with vegetables. The temple was open to the elements. It was normal in summer to meditate in a cloud of biting mosquitoes and in the winter to freeze. Many of the monks suffered from frostbite. Shinzan lost half an ear in the cold. Amid the rigours, however, he flourished. The old suffering slipped away. His heart became clearer and happier. He directly experienced "*sen shin*"—the purification of the heart.

We come through all the twists and turns of his life to his 80th year. During that half-century of Zen practice Shinzan Rōshi has put a lot of work into going deeper himself and helping many other people with their development as well. In marking his 80th year, it is significant that he has brushed this phrase a number of times. I visited Gyokuryuji in January 2015 and there it was hanging in pride of place in the tearoom: "*sen*" meaning "washing" or "purifying", and "*shin*", "the heart". The book that changed his life, and this process of purifying the heart has clearly been in his mind recently.

In the process of finding our truth, purifying the heart is very important. It is something that we do not often explore that much in the west. One of the reasons why is because we have a tendency to be very hard on ourselves. There are accounts of the Dalai Lama when he first started to teach westerners being absolutely bowled over by the fact that so many of them basically did not like themselves. This was something completely beyond his experience. Why that is of significance will emerge in a moment.

In Zen, this process of purifying the heart is called in Japanese "*sange*" (pronounced san-gay). Of the two characters in the term "*sange*", the first, "*san*", literally means to "recognise" or "acknowledge" the past and what we have done in the past; "*ge*" means to "resolve to do differently in the future". So essentially when we practise meditation seriously, we come to face ourselves squarely. One of the things that will arise in that honest clarity is we start to see things we have done and that have happened to us in the past that are out of harmony with our true nature.

If we do not turn away, and if we really allow all the negative aspects of ourselves to arise, then within that clarity arises the motivation to adjust our lives, to shift course in such a way that we live in ways more resonant with our true nature.

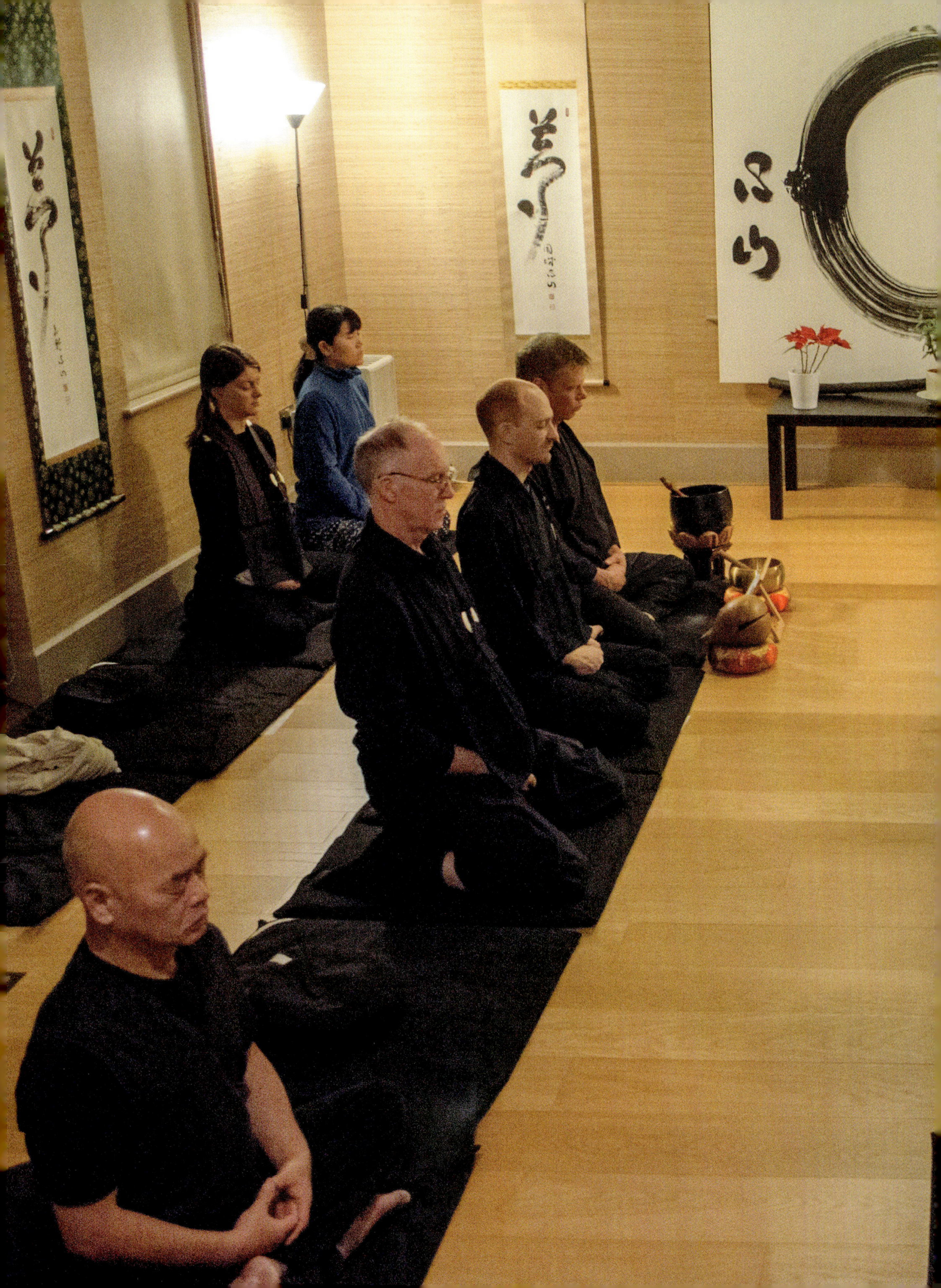

Zazen at Yugagyo Dōjō in Camberwell, London

So *sange* is a recognition and a changing of course. And this process, this *sange*, typically starts with the gross elements and becomes more and more subtle as time goes on. I think we can view it as a lifelong process. With his 50 years of Zen practice Shinzan Rōshi is still reflecting on this purifying of the heart.

Now it is so easy for us westerners with the orientation that we do not fundamentally like ourselves to take this the wrong way—to use this process as a stick with which to beat ourselves. That is not the point at all. It is actually much more about taking ourselves sufficiently seriously, and giving ourselves the best chance to really move forward into a new life.

In the Zen process of purifying the heart, when you are willing to open yourself to those areas of which perhaps you might not be so proud, those areas that perhaps aren't your best, those that you would rather others didn't know about—in that opening you are actually opening yourself to that which is beyond human limitation. As we open ourselves to all the foibles of our human nature, we simultaneously open ourselves to the vastness of our Buddha Nature. You find who you really are. You find your true basis.

In this process you remain, as far as I can tell, from the beginning to the end, a human being with all the idiosyncrasies, limitations and weaknesses of our humanity. They don't go away. But we start to see more and more clearly that we don't have to act on them. We actually have a foot in two worlds. We have a foot in the world of our human nature and we have a foot in the world of our Buddha nature. And actually these form one world, not two worlds.

We can view the process of living out the truth of Zen practice as the process of bringing together heaven and earth. This starts to happen and continues to happen through purifying the heart, through this ongoing *sange*, this ongoing practice.

In the ceremony of formally taking the precepts, this process of *sange*, this process of purification, this process of acknowledging the past and resolving or clarifying the way forward into the future is enshrined. But you don't have to wait for any ceremony, you can start now.

Just coming to sit down, being willing to face yourself, *sange* happens. We are beckoning to it. Just be open to absolutely whatever arises: your human nature, your Buddha nature. If you open yourself to all of it without censorship, without avoidance, you will touch enlightenment. It is not necessarily a long process to get the first definite sense of who and how you really are. You can do it today. It is just a matter of facing yourself fully. In repeatedly brushing this calligraphy, Shinzan Rōshi makes it clear that this is his wish for you.

Enso – Look at Nature, Become Buddha

The second piece of work I want to look at is the traditional *enso* or Zen "empty circle". In this example (pictured here, also see p50) Shinzan Rōshi has written in English "Look at Nature Become Buddha". Let us explore some aspects of this.

It is unusual for a Zen calligrapher to write in English, but not unprecedented. Nakagawa Soen Rōshi (1907–1984), former teacher at Ryutakuji, spent considerable time in the United States and was very playful in his calligraphy. He sometimes used English. These days, Vietnamese Zen master Thich Nhat Hanh sometimes uses English in his calligraphy too.

Shinzan Rōshi's increasing interest in using the brush and ink to write in English, and to lead calligraphy workshops, has deep roots in his life. We mentioned his early meeting with the American soldier in the immediate aftermath of the war. This meeting, and a growing interest in baseball, made the young man keen to pursue his study of English. Eventually he would travel to teach Zen in the United States, Canada and Europe. There are some other aspects of this openness to the West that Shinzan Rōshi has demonstrated that we will explore shortly, but first let us look at the content of what he has written.

This "Look at Nature Become Buddha" is actually part of a four-phrase summary of the essence of Zen, attributed to Daruma (Bodhidharma), the Indian monk who brought the Zen tradition, so we are told, from India to China. The full text runs,

> "A direct transmission outside the scriptures.
> No reliance on words and letters.
> Looking directly into the human heart.
> Seeing your true nature and becoming Buddha."

So the Zen tradition claims to embody this direct transmission, this "passing on of the flame", if you like, from torch to torch, from teacher to student down through the centuries. The real thing is not based on learning or ordination or years of seniority, but on direct realisation and the following generation attaining the same realisation.

Within Zen our primary field of study, rather than being words and letters or scriptures, is the human heart, ourselves. This assertion goes right back to the Buddha, when he states that the whole path is found "In this very one-fathom-long body, along with its perceptions and thoughts."

So within yourself you find your truth, your liberation, your enlightenment. This process of finding your enlightenment in Japanese is called *kenshō*—seeing your true nature. When you thoroughly and deeply see who you are, your true nature, you become Buddha.

There is only one kind of enlightenment. Shinzan Rōshi often uses the image of a dirty window. When you clean the window, the light shines through. It is the same light whether we clean a little corner, or clear the whole thing. There are, thus, different degrees or intensities of this one light, and in practice everyone seems to go through an enlightening process as more and more light penetrates.

Two and a half thousand years ago, the Buddha himself went through this *kenshō* process. He studied himself in depth and detail and when he had gone far enough in that study, he realised the truth of himself. In doing that, he realised the truth of all things. As he woke up, the Zen tradition has him saying:

> "I am enlightened together with the whole earth and all its sentient beings."

So this calligraphy points to the heart of Zen and the root of Buddhism. Shinzan Rōshi indirectly incorporates the above quotation within his translation of this key Zen phrase, coming up with the wonderfully ambiguous: "Look at nature become Buddha". Also implied is his passionate advocacy of the natural environment. He places this phrase within the famous Zen *enso* or empty circle.

The empty circle points to a certain phase in practice. During your study of the human heart, at a certain point a shift occurs. For a moment, the lights blink off and then they blink on again. We have a discontinuity. And there is really nothing you can say about this shift because there is no *you* there.

We have these shifts all the time in many different contexts. You have a shift when you sneeze! It is hard to talk about the direct experience of sneezing. So it is not that *kenshō* is terribly rarefied—people sometimes make it a terribly grand and wondrous and mysterious thing. It is not. But there is this kind of shift, this discontinuity and, because you cannot say anything about it, it is often depicted as an empty circle. And it is important that you practise far enough that you get this shift.

With his own practice, Shinzan Rōshi was a late starter. He had come to practice later than the other monks in the monastery, and was about 30 when he fully engaged. He had a burning desire to find a real basis to his life after his business failures. When he was met by Itsugai Rōshi's closed door, he felt somewhat stymied. But this just increased his determination to practise, trying to find the truth, trying to get this shift, this *kenshō*.

Itsugai recognised his sincerity of purpose and relented. He urged Shinzan onwards. The young monk practised even harder, frequently deep into the night. One particular night, he was meditating in the small hours and he left his body. This can happen, sometimes. A meditator can get to the point where it feels like they are a consciousness completely separated from their body.

What happens when you experience this is suddenly you realise, "Gosh! Even if my body is crushed by a car or falls off a cliff, I am still fine. In fact I feel better than when I'm in my body." And so a whole raft of fear melts away. So much of the fear that we carry around in life is around the wellbeing of our body. When we suddenly realise, "It doesn't matter. My body really doesn't matter. I am fine," then all this fear just melts away.

So this happened to Shinzan. He went into *sanzen* and laid out to Itsugai Rōshi what had happened.

Itsugai thundered, "No, no, no, that is not *kenshō*. That is not it." But Shinzan was absolutely certain that he had found what he was looking for. This intoxicating sense of fearlessness can be very convincing.

So Shinzan carried on going to *sanzen*. He was doing quite well with his interviews and going on in his practice. Itsugai Rōshi was not somebody you could argue with, but nevertheless there was a question mark in Shinzan's heart. He was sure he had found what he had been looking for. Why couldn't the Zen master see?

Of course, Itsugai Rōshi could see very clearly. This kind of experience is not unusual. The Tibetans have a practice in which they learn to consciously do this. Essentially they rehearse how to die and they learn how to leave the body at will. Many people experience this sort of thing when they are very ill. It can also happen when you've had a serious injury. It can happen through deep meditation, but it is not *kenshō*. This is a false *kenshō*. It is an *experience*, which is not what Bodhidharma, the great master, was pointing to in his phrase of "Seeing your true nature and becoming Buddha."

Similarly, people sometimes get deceived by experiences of light, or bliss or exaltation. There is nothing wrong with any of these things, but it is the nature of experiences, however sublime, to wear off. What we find in *kenshō* does not wear off, it doesn't come and doesn't go. Experiences of all kinds, positive and negative, are absolutely no problem at all. The problem comes when we identify with them. Then we stop moving forward. And for a little time Shinzan did that, but Itsugai Rōshi was a good teacher, saw what was happening and urged him on with promises that there was more to find.

Shinzan pushed on in his practice. One night he was practising with the koan "mu" up on the mountain behind Shōgenji. He shouted "*Muuuuuuuu!*" with his entire being. In talking about the incident later, he simply said, "I lost myself." Itsugai recognised this genuine *kenshō* and to this day Shinzan Rōshi remains deeply grateful for the master's compassion and skill.

So the difference between the previous disembodiment, the leaving the body experience and a genuine *kenshō* is that the *kenshō* is not in itself an experience. It is a shift in the way that you relate to all experiences.

You don't need to leave your body to get the shift. You don't need to have any particular experience happen. It is very possible to have this shift happen when you are being miserable, when you are feeling tired, when you are feeling completely ordinary. It can happen at times when your meditation is particularly deep, but not necessarily. For many people there is a concentrated period of meditation. And then it is afterwards when they are relaxing, when they are frying some chips or driving home in the car suddenly completely unbidden this shift comes along. Both you and the world are both exactly the same before and after, but your interpretation shifts.

So eventually Shinzan underwent this shift. But that was just the beginning. A first *kenshō* is simply an entrance to the gateway of Zen. Master Hakuin, the great reformer of the Rinzai school, strongly emphasised continuing *kōan* study leading to further *kenshōs* and an ever-deepening understanding. Under Itsugai Rōshi, Shinzan studied the hundreds of *kōans* of the Mino branch of the Inzan lineage. Any attempt at an intellectual understanding of these old cases would have him thrown out of the *sanzen* room. The emphasis was on becoming a fool—becoming the *kōan* itself and deepening the direct non-mediated understanding. Once he had passed the *kōans* and further matured his understanding, he began to teach.

In my experience of him, Shinzan Rōshi has very much always focused on the sincerity of the person in front of him. If you want to achieve this shift, if you want to find this unshakeable basis to your life, the key requisite is this sincerity of heart. Everything else in a sense is negotiable. It doesn't really matter how intelligent you are or how good a life you have led or how healthy you are—there are certain things that can help, but essentially, if you really want to do it, you can. This sincerity of heart is really central.

Back in 2011 when we opened our training hall in London, Shinzan Rōshi came over from Japan to preside and many students were present at the talk he gave. One of the things he said was, "I am expecting the Zen masters of the future to come from this hall. Why? Because there is no money, there is no fame to be had in this business over in the UK. People are coming here for the right reasons. And when they have the right reasons, then everything else automatically follows."

He was deadly serious. He is expecting Zen masters of the future to come from the West. There are certain problems with Zen in Japan these days where some people are coming to Zen with other motivations that are not leading to this shift, to this *kenshō* or finding your true nature. But over here we are finding lots of people are doing this and it can deeply transform and enrich their lives. And each person who does this finds their true nature upholds this lineage, this direct transmission outside the scriptures.

I remember Shinzan Rōshi saying to me that he had noticed how the progress of Zen had always been in an eastward direction moving from India to China from China to Japan and then going further east from Japan to what we call the West. In Sōtō Zen one of the key poems that they chant every morning begins, "From West to East unseen flowed out the mind of India's greatest sage and to the source kept true as an unsullied stream is clear." Shinzan Rōshi has written this calligraphy in English to make the point that this eastward flowing is actually happening and he wants to support that. He wants to affirm the reality of this flowing out of the true mind of India's greatest sage, the true mind of Buddha. So our part within this is really to look into the human heart, to study ourselves deeply. When we do this, the rest follows.

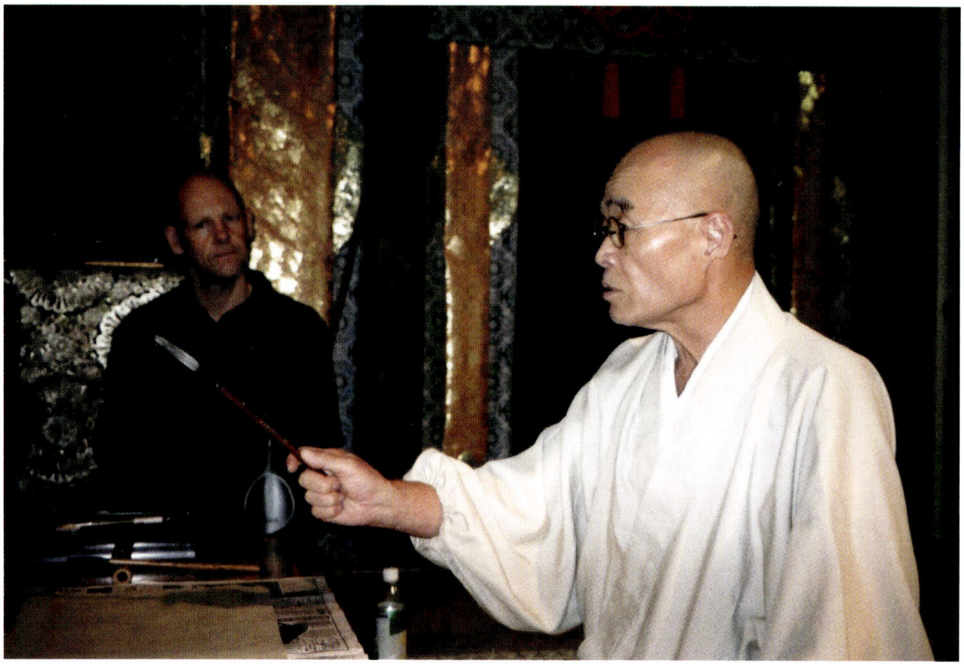

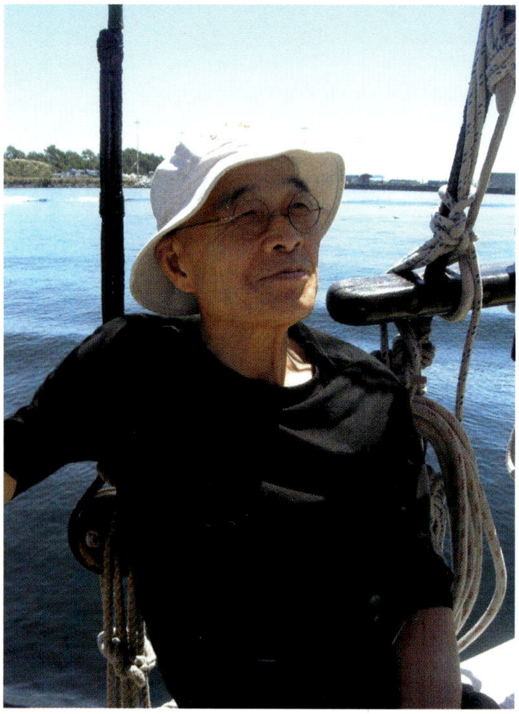

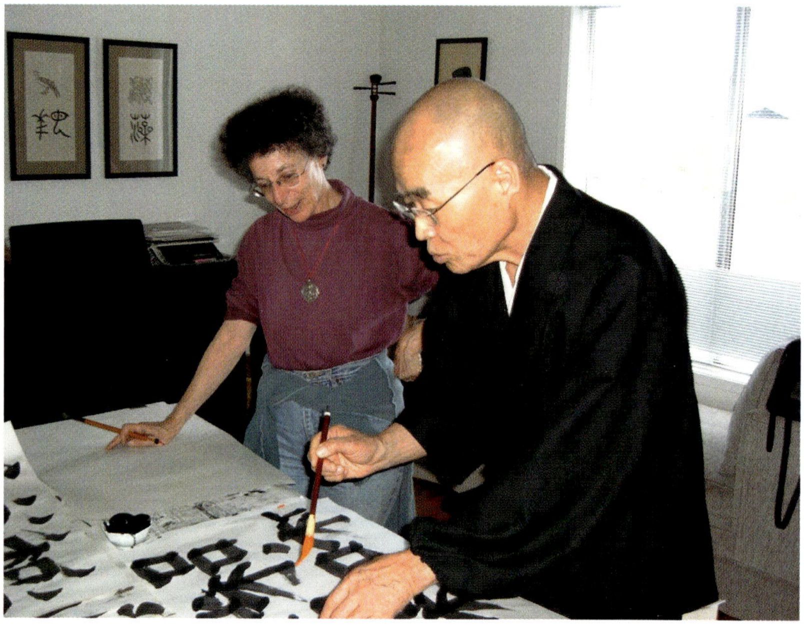

© 木法
月 BAERNDAL

Yume – Dream

What is your dream? This is the question inspiring the calligraphy of the single Japanese character *"yume"* (p64). The flow of brush strokes have the meaning of the word "dream".

You will notice that this particular calligraphy pictured here has been burned. There is also some water damage. It was rescued from a fire at Gyokuryuji—but that comes later in our story.

When we think of this word "dream" in English, we can have a sense of something that we wish to happen, something we want to achieve—perhaps a goal or an intention. It could also be the kind of dream that arises spontaneously when you are asleep, and the daydreams we have when we are awake. So the English term "vision" would also be encompassed by this one character. All these meanings are reflected in *"yume"*.

The famous Buddhist text, the Diamond Sutra, says you should regard the world as a dream. When I talked to Shinzan Rōshi about this calligraphy, this was his primary source. Sometimes people think that this teaching means that we should look on everything as unreal and as though nothing is true, but it is not quite like that. It is a little more that our fixed perception of things might not be all it seems.

Zen often refers to the Chinese philosopher, Chuang-tzu, who has a little story that is very famous in east Asia. He recounts falling asleep and having a dream. He dreams he is a butterfly and then, on waking up, he is not sure whether he is Chuang-tzu, who has just dreamt that he is a butterfly, or whether he is a butterfly dreaming that he is Chuang-tzu. When we look on the world and our experience of it, we tend to make things very solid, very real—it is part of what we do as humans. Sometimes we are not aware that we are creating this solidity.

Eventually, however, we might start to notice that so-called solid things have a kind of evanescent or flowing or dream-like quality about them. We can see that our perceiving of them contributes greatly to their being there at all.

Science continues to explore this as well. Physicists tell us that, if you look at anything closely enough, it is a fizz of atomic or subatomic particles moving very fast, in which everything is both a particle and a wave, even moving in and out of "existence". The eye of meditation detects something very similar. When you clarify your vision, things are not as fixed as they previously seemed—and that includes you.

There are many ramifications of this but one of them is that reality is very changeable. We all know that different people experience the same reality in very different ways. To somebody who is used to a very luxurious, cossetted lifestyle, our Zen training hall might seem quite stark and functional, but somebody coming from almost any previous century would think this is a very comfortable place with its controlled heating and lighting, water on tap and cushions to sit on.

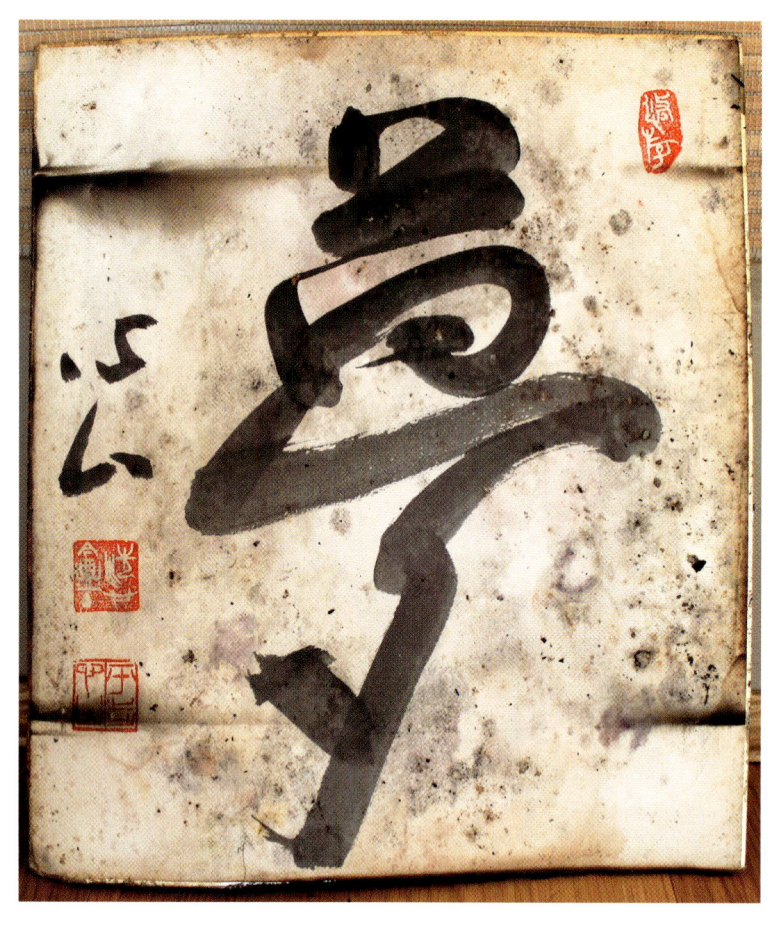

As we live in our own dream, experiencing our own reality, we can come to see that we have a point of freedom within our perception of things. Reality is much more malleable than we might initially think. So the quality of "*yume*", or "dream" (as in direction, or intention in your life) becomes very important. What is your dream? In what direction do you wish to steer the course of your life. Where do you want it to go?

Shinzan Rōshi, when he became a Zen monk after entering Shōgenji, his very strict Zen training monastery, studied very seriously and formed his dream. His intention. What he wanted more than anything else, was to find the deeper basis to life and make it available to others.

One of the things he realised when he was in training was that not everyone had the same dream or intention. Many of the young monks in the temple were only there for a minimum period of two or three years or even less. They were essentially doing a set amount of time in the temple so that they could be certified and go back to their home temples in their villages, where they mainly presided over funerals. At the time, and to the present day, there was money to be made performing funerals, so probably most of the young trainee monks did not have any great intentions to plumb the depths of their hearts. There were, however, others in the temple who were practising seriously, and with sincerity—but they were in a minority. So there was this kind of dual purpose going on within the training monastery.

One day in the *sanzen* room, Itsugai Rōshi looked intently at Shinzan and said: "As surely as my pupils are black, you are worthy to be Zen master of Shōgenji." He recognised Shinzan's spiritual attainment. However, at that point he did not give him the Zen master's paperwork.

Soon afterwards, Itsugai Rōshi became abbot of the head temple, Myoshinji in Kyoto. His intention was for Shinzan to go through the ceremonial formalities to become a Zen master with another senior monk. Despite many years of monastery experience, this man had not yet opened his spiritual eye. Shinzan could not do it. He felt that he would be living a lie and that receiving authentication paperwork from this person would be meaningless.

So Shinzan went to study with another Zen master, making his misgivings public. In so doing, he made an enemy. It was only many years later that there was a rapprochement between the two monks.

Continuing his dream of living from this deeper basis to life, Shinzan moved to a tiny temple deep in the mountains called Enjoji. He continued his Zen study at nearby Kokutaiji monastery with a very good teacher called Inaba Shinden. In time, Shinden Rōshi wanted Shinzan to be his successor at Kokutaiji, but when he died, the old enemy that Shinzan had left behind at the previous temple made sure that this intention was blocked.

This was a time of clarifying the dream. Broadly there are three kinds of Zen temple in Japan. There are local temples by and large concerned with funerals, and frequently these days in the hands of a temple family in which the father of the family acts as the priest and his son is trained to become the successor.

Then there are monasteries that could perhaps more properly called seminaries. Typically they are occupied by a majority of junior monks or trainees who are there to earn the certification necessary to inherit their fathers' temple, together with some more long-term practitioners.

Then there are a few hermitage temples that are largely outside the mainstream.

At this time in his life, Shinzan Rōshi realised he did not want to run a training school for funeral priests. He had discovered Gyokuryuji, former hermitage of the great Zen master Bankei, while out on *takuhatsu* (alms round). The little temple had no source of income and had thus been long abandoned. The buildings that remained were on the point of collapse. Shinzan Rōshi moved in and began saving what was left. As he restored the hermitage, he dreamed of restoring the focus of the Zen school. He put up a sign at the gate announcing, "Training place for both young and old people to come and realise awakening." This was much more in line with his dream.

He taught very actively and very assiduously, as he does to this day. He would give a talk every morning and very often he would start his talk, "The first priority is *kenshō* (seeing your true nature). The second priority is *kenshō*. The third priority is *kenshō*." He took it upon himself to emphasise this earnest seeking and to reach out to people who wished to find who they really were and live from this deeper basis.

I experienced this immediately as I joined the little community that formed around Shinzan Rōshi. I was assigned to work with Morimoto-san, the temple carpenter. Just before I arrived he had had a powerful *kenshō*. His shining eyes overflowed with love and kindness. Everything he did was for the benefit of others. We spent months working together up on the temple roof and then a big earthquake hit a town in northern Japan. Morimoto-san's dream was to go to help in the rebuilding effort.

In helping people to find their *yume*, Shinzan Rōshi emphasised the teachings of two previous Zen masters. He spoke with reverence of Bankei, the founder of the hermitage where we lived. Unquestionably the most popular Zen master in Japanese history, Bankei's simple teaching involved pointing out to people the truth of their being, in the moment. "Don't wait to become a Buddha," he would say. "Simply be a Buddha right now."

In contrast to this gentle approach were the teachings of fiery Zen master Hakuin. Tirelessly exhorting his students to find the clear-cut breakthrough of *kenshō*, Hakuin was a freelance like Shinzan Rōshi. He operated from Shoinji, a tiny temple in a village at the foot of Mount Fuji. His influence was such that monks and lay students from all over Japan spilled out from Shoinji to turn the whole surrounding landscape into a Zen *dōjō*, or training centre. Hakuin emphasised intense meditative focus on a *kōan*, or spiritual question, coupled with special practices to ground and energise the body.

Shinzan Rōshi's teachings were kaleidoscopic, drawing freely from these two great Zen masters. His dream, his intention, was to share what he had found, and he lived and lives according to what he believes to be right. In contrast to the routines of the monasteries, the hermitage style of practice means he can be very free and fluid, making each moment a teaching. I came to him after a decade and a half of Zen monastery practice with all the inevitable habits and rigidities of being institutionalised for so long. He delighted in breaking down these rigidities in me, constantly challenging me with the unexpected.

When you come to practice meditation, part of what you are doing is searching your heart, finding the dreamlike or evanescent quality to everything, and uncovering what you truly wish for. If you are willing to pay the price, your dream will most likely be yours. If we follow through on this, our dream becomes the gate to our true nature, our Buddha nature. A true dream expresses this true nature and thus brings great benefit to ourselves, and great benefit to the world.

Chu-dō – The Middle Way

In my time studying with Shinzan Rōshi, I have often heard him discuss "the middle way" or "*chu-dō*", and here he has brushed the term (as pictured below, and described in detail on p74). "*Chu-dō*" is made up of two characters—the top one is "*chu*", which means "centre" or "middle". Beneath it is "*dō*", which means "way" or "road". Within Buddhism, the middle way has many resonances.

Two and a half thousand years ago, the Buddha-to-be was born into a very luxurious and pampered background. His family, particularly his father, went to great lengths to keep him isolated. In his early twenties the young man experienced life outside the palace for the first time and was profoundly shocked. He realised he had been living a fantasy and this shock spurred him into leaving home. Many yogis in the Buddha's time lived and experimented with spiritual practices in the solitude of the forests, and this was where he was drawn. Popular practices of the time involved depriving the physical body in a quest to reveal the soul.

The young man joined the forest yogis and after trying meditation, experimented with practices such as the "Five Fires", where four bonfires are built close together, the fifth fire being the noonday sun overhead. The practitioner sits between these fires trying to "cook" himself to liberation.

He explored a range of these yogic methods, and settled on fasting. The old texts talk about him getting to the point of eating one grain of rice a day and almost shrinking away to nothing.

Eventually he realised that harming of his body was not setting anything free. The further he went down this road of pain and deprivation, the more dull and slow his mind was becoming. He came to the end of the road of extremism.

At this point the story places him beside a river called the Nerañjarā, which is a tributary of the Ganges. A boat with a musician on board floats into view. The musician is playing a vina, which is a rather like a guitar or lute. Its top string was wound up incredibly tightly, and when played, it snapped instantly. The bottom string, in contrast, was so loose that, when played, no sound could be heard from it. The middle string, at a medium tension, could actually produce the music.

It is not clear whether this experience was an actual event or a vision, but the principle of the middle way between self-indulgence and self-deprivation powerfully influenced the young seeker in his practice, and in his successful finding of enlightenment, and later in his teaching.

In the second and third century AD a profound school

Gyokuryuji, near Seki, central Japan

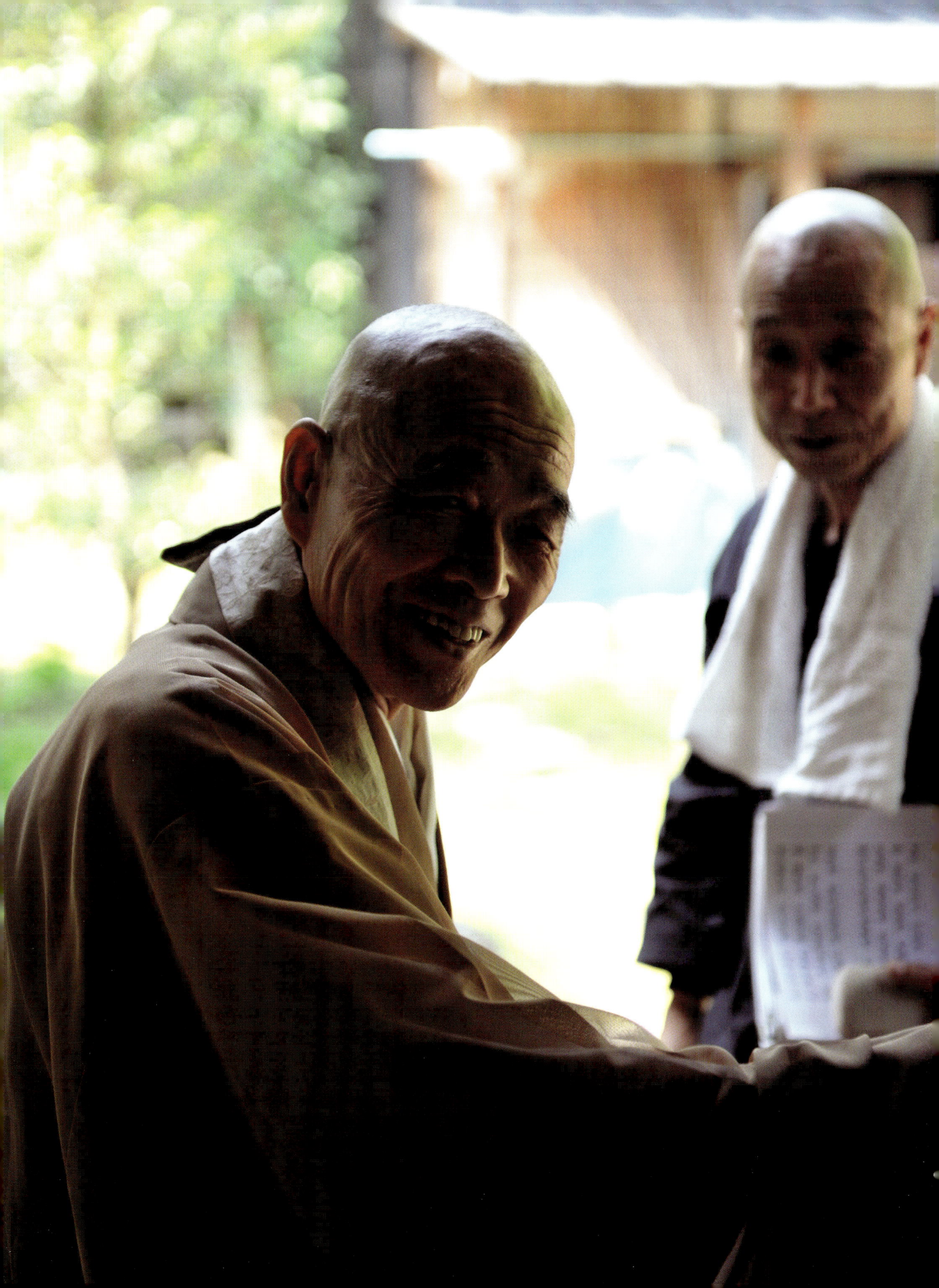

of Buddhist philosophy called the Madhyamika, or Middle Way, arose. This posed a middle way between the views of eternalism and nihilism.

Eternalism stems from the view that things are fixed, solid and unchanging—the human core or soul exists forever. Nihilism is the position that nothing really exists and everything is an illusion. All that human beings are left with is futility and meaninglessness.

The middle way is called in Sanskrit "*śūnyatā*" or "emptiness". Reality is a flowing dance of change. There are ultimately no things, simply processes. In our quantum physics-influenced world, it is much easier for us to grasp this point than it was for the ancients.

The Buddha himself urged that, rather than relying on hearsay or rites and rituals, we set our lives in order, live ethically, and investigate reality for ourselves. When start to do this, we can directly perceive that things are much less fixed, much less concrete than they first appear. So the commonplace view of the world as being a place full of separate objects, everything solid and unchanging, starts to melt.

Related to this, Zen, in common with many approaches to spiritual development, has a sense that the human organism is an energetic phenomenon. This energy or vitality can be elevated or depleted. This notion of the Middle Way has energetic ramifications.

There is a middle way or middle road running right through the centre of your being and there is an intimate connection between your energy and your conscious state. Down through the centuries, generations of meditators have explored this. You can change your consciousness by changing your energy, and vice versa.

Most of the energy routes or channels in the body have an opposite. For example, there is a meridian that runs down the front of the body, and a corresponding channel running down the back. There are major left and right ones, and so on. But there is a central one that has no opposites. It runs right through the core of your body. When your energy enters this central core, the corresponding consciousness also has no opposites. It is a consciousness that is not based on separation or duality.

In the world of this and that, of subject and object, we are always in a vulnerable position. This is the world of life and death, success and failure. But in this non-separate or non-dual consciousness, we enter a place where we have no problems. Your true centre is actually the centre of the universe. In this place you have everything, and in fact you are everything.

The very posture of your body in meditation when you are relaxed, balanced, upright and open, encourages your conscious awareness and energy to settle into this middle way. Shinzan Rōshi brushed this calligraphy from this place and intends to concretely depict it.

When I lived with him, one of the things that was a central feature of life in the temple was that he was very open to all sorts of people coming—particularly people who were struggling in life. It seemed as though the more troubled people were, the more he wanted to extend a welcome to them. So we had people who were crazy, or homeless, or part of the mafia! No one was excluded. Sometimes I imagined it must have been a little bit like living with Jesus, who also seemed very comfortable spending his time with people who did not really fit in with society.

For example, Japan has a very tough education system. Some children find it too much: they can't keep up, they don't fit in and some of them end up living in seclusion in their bedrooms, sometimes for years. They are called *hikikomori*, and every so often one of these children or young people might feel desperate enough to harm or kill family members. People in their communities become afraid of them, creating deeper isolation. Shinzan Rōshi was very keen to welcome *hikikomori* and other outcasts to try to help them find a way back into society.

For those of us training in the temple, we had to learn to work with these people and still maintain the schedule. Things could get quite wild, even sometimes dangerous! Of all the people who came to the temple, the most controversial were former members of a Japanese cult called Aum Shinrikyo. The cult developed the idea that Armageddon was coming, and if they could cause greater chaos within society, then the end of the world would be accelerated, finally breaking through into a happy future. The cult stockpiled weapons, viruses like ebola and various toxic chemicals. They got to the point in 1995 of manufacturing the deadly poison gas Sarin, and releasing it on the Tokyo subway killing 12 people and injuring many more.

People were absolutely terrified of this cult. Many of the former Aum Shinrikyo members arriving at Gyokuryuji had been put through brainwashing methods, including high doses of LSD, electric shock treatments, immersion in scalding water, and other practices far from the middle way. It was extremely difficult for them to readjust back to normal life. Also the climate of fear around them meant that it was difficult to get even the simplest or lowest-level job. Shinzan Rōshi welcomed these people into the temple with open arms, and helped them to readjust into society.

Of the entire group, the person who was most feared and reviled within Japan was the leader, Shoko Asahara, who is in prison and on trial at this time. Possibly the second was senior member Kazuaki Okazaki. Before the poison gas incident, a Japanese anti-cult lawyer had written articles critical of Aum Shinrikyo. Okuzaki broke into the lawyer's apartment with accomplices, and murdered him, his wife and their young child.

He turned himself in to the police and admitted his guilt. However, Okazaki was so indoctrinated that he was absolutely certain what he had done was right. The cult deprogrammers could not find any chink in his armour.

Shinzan Rōshi became involved in Okuzaki's rehabilitation—and he took a different approach. He engaged him on the level of his meditation practice by asking about his personal experiences. Shinzan Rōshi validated some of what he had experienced but pointed out that there was so much more. Surprisingly there was a breakthrough. This brainwashed and very fixed character started to soften and open, seeing beyond his indoctrination and moving towards the middle way.

Shinzan Rōshi visited Okazaki regularly in prison. Gradually the prisoner started to recognise his awful crime. He began to try to do his very best to make amends, making apologies to surviving family members. He became a student of Shinzan Rōshi and studied Zen with him. A gifted artist, his Zen-inspired drawing regularly appeared in Gyokuryuji magazine at the time (an example is pictured here).

As Okazaki's trial progressed he eventually received the death sentence; he was the first of the Aum Shinrikyo members to do so. Under Japanese law he was only permitted to receive visits from family members. So Shinzan Rōshi took steps towards adopting this hated man so that he could continue his visits. You can imagine the ripples this caused in every aspect of Shinzan's life. His wife divorced him and many people in the Zen establishment shook their heads. Shinzan Rōshi continued.

On the 5 November 2005, we had a very sudden aggressive fire at Gyokuryuji that burned down half of the temple in about 40 minutes. In the immediate aftermath of this fire, rumours abounded. Some supposed that the fire had been caused by existing members of the Aum Shinrikyo cult who were angry at Shinzan Rōshi for helping former members get away and start new lives, and even practice Zen.

There were also rumours that the fire had been started by people who were opposed to, and afraid of, Aum Shinrikyo—that the fire was an act of revenge. It was a fearful and unstable time in the temple. And winter arrived soon after. We had no kitchen, no water supply, no bathhouse and no office. More than half of our little community left over the winter months.

Eventually it was discovered that the fire was started by a young boy who was staying in the temple and had been playing with matches.

The fire consumed everything Shinzan Rōshi owned. On his computer was a new book about the middle way he had just finished writing (he had already published a couple of other books). The new book, together with all his back-up discs, were completely destroyed.

Drawing by Kazuaki Okazaki, Shinzan Rōshi's student on death row.

Right in the middle of the chaos as we were working with the fire hoses, I remember him walking behind me and I clearly heard him say four words in English, "Everything gone, but OK." It was absolutely true. In the aftermath of all of the fear, chaos and destruction, he simply carried straight on. Although he lost a couple of years' work on the book, we have in this calligraphy a distillation of all the teaching and meaning of *chu-dō*, the middle way.

When talking with Shinzan Rōshi about this scroll, it was very clear that his deepest wish is that every person who comes to Zen finds this middle way, this true centre that has no opposites. This the place where you find a happiness that nobody can give you, and that nobody can ever take away from you. When we come to sit in meditation, we invite the dawning of this new consciousness, we settle into the middle way.

True Person of No Rank

Master Rinzai stood up before the assembly and said: "There is a true person of no rank coming and going through the gates of your senses. New students who have not yet witnessed this, look! Look!"

Rinzai (?-866 CE) is the foundational Zen master of our school, and this particular very short piece of teaching brushed by Shinzan Rōshi (as shown below and described in detail on p98) captures his fundamental emphasis. He had the reputation of being a very dynamic teacher. He was famous for being very attuned to his students and able to shout at exactly the right moment to enable them to let go and wake up.

Anyone who has spent any length of time with our teacher in Japan, Shinzan Rōshi, will have heard this phrase "true person" or "true man". He constantly uses it to refer to the goal of our practice. In Shinzan Rōshi's own life he has constantly stepped away from rank and position. As he turned his attention away from the priest-training establishments, he naturally focused on "*zaike bukkyo*", or lay Buddhism.

There is no single Rinzai school in Japan; instead there are 15 self-standing branches or factions. Soon after my arrival to practise with Shinzan Rōshi, in 2002 or 2003, I remember him writing a letter to the Myoshinji faction to formally withdraw Gyokuryuji (his temple in Seki, central Japan). As part of his activities he had continued to rail against the inflated prices that were being charged within the entire Japanese Buddhist world for funerals. The situation became so bad that a satirical movie "Osohiki" ("The Funeral") depicted a Buddhist priest arriving to conduct a funeral in his white Rolls Royce. Shinzan Rōshi responded by teaching lay students how to conduct low-cost funerals within their own communities. Subsequent complaints from funeral priests made staying within the Myoshinji fold problematic. Some time after his withdrawal, when he was in his seventies, the Myoshinji administration of the time responded by formally expelling him, cutting off his pension and draining the temple bank account. These days Shinzan Rōshi has no connection with funerals at all.

There have been several lay-based Zen organisations in Japanese history. In recent years the *Ningen Zen Kyōdan*, with 15 lay Zen masters, has spread throughout Japan, and the *Sambō Kyōdan*, as well having an impact on Japanese Zen, has been highly influential in the USA. These organisations have in common a focus on direct realisation and a disassociation from funeral Buddhism. In this context, Shinzan Rōshi gave his blessing to the founding of *Zendō Kyōdan* (Zenways Community), which is aimed at fostering human awakening and wellbeing within the conditions of modern life. He also has independent successors in Japan, Tomio Yugaku Ameku, and in Canada, Eshin Melody Cornell.

As of now, Shinzan Rōshi continues his Zen practice at Gyokuryuji, living as a hermit accompanied by his beloved dogs. Still to this day (I was with him most recently in March 2015) this phrase, Rinzai's "true person" or "true man," was pretty much constantly on his lips. Why is this so important?

When we go through the stages of human development, if all goes well, we arrive at the state of adulthood. An adult is somebody who the law, our society and our culture deems is in a position to manage their own affairs and take responsibility for themselves. In order for somebody to take this position, or rank, of adulthood, they have to have a clear sense of themselves. This sense of "me", in contradistinction to the rest of the world, is a characteristic of the adult worldview or mind state.

This world view is true, worthwhile and very valuable. Through the hardening or sharpening of the sense of "this is me, that is the world", this ability to make distinctions, we have become a great success as a species. We have colonised this planet pretty much from pole to pole. We have taken over all the good land. Even in less developed areas, we put tremendous energy into creating the best possible environments for ourselves to flourish and reproduce.

But when we only have this view of, "this is me, that is the world", this separated view, then always we are in a precarious position. The world is so much bigger than me. I am limited—limited in time, limited in space. Of course there is a great deal we do to overcome our limitations—we fly through the air, we go under the sea, we can preserve food and create benign environments—we can do so many things to make life more possible and extend our range. But extending our limits, however far it goes, is just that—an extension. And with every extension of our human limits comes a price tag.

With the adult, or separated mind set, many of us close our eyes to this price. Nevertheless, the cost is unavoidable. Shinzan Rōshi's birthplace, Fukushima, recently experienced the largest peacetime nuclear disaster, ranking alongside Chernobyl at grade 7 on the nuclear disaster scale. The area within a 20 kilometre-plus radius around the power station was sealed off, and we will not know the long-term effects for generations. So it is perhaps understandable that, when you meet Shinzan Rōshi, you will soon find out that he is very concerned about the prices we pay for the extension of our human limits.

When we live a separated or isolated life, it is natural to think in terms of our own lifespan. It is easy to decide that if things don't change too much during our own 80 or 90 years, perhaps all is basically well. If the planet is going to be a little bit damaged during our lifetime, perhaps it does not matter that much. If the scientists tell us that we are losing at least one species every single day, but we don't directly see it, perhaps it is not such a big deal.

This limiting of our view has become critical. We are getting to the point now where human beings will either shift their consciousness and expand beyond this view, or very likely become extinct. We will make this environment sufficiently damaged so that it cannot support us any longer. We become victims of our own over-success.

We can contrast this "adult" world view with the teachings of Master Rinzai and the teachings of Shinzan Rōshi: "There is a true person of no rank coming and going through the gates of your senses." When we think of the adult world view, we are in the world of rank, of position—essentially the world of comparison—"I am above that person, I am below that person. That species is less important than me. This situation is more important than that situation." This is the world of comparison, or the world of this and that, the world of separation.

Master Rinzai is holding up another view—there is a true person of no rank coming and going through the gates of your senses. You will notice he talks about this true person coming and going. The adult world view or mind set is based on a very separated view: this is me; that's the world. This true person view involves coming and going, a dynamic interrelationship with the environment, with the world. The true person isn't separate from the entire world. The true you is inseparable from your environment. It makes no sense from this viewpoint to harm your environment—you are only harming yourself. Shinzan Rōshi deeply believes that the only hope for our species on this planet is for enough people to wake up to this true view and become true people.

One of the things about us human beings is it only takes a relatively small number of influential people to have a disproportionate degree of influence. If even perhaps one or two per cent of the population could really live from this viewpoint of being a true person, of really grounding themselves in this reality in which the inner and the outer are simply mirrors reflecting each other, then our problems would vanish. We would not only survive but would flourish in this environment we find ourselves in. This environment, rather than becoming a used-up rubbish tip, would become the paradise that it really is.

Even though these days Shinzan Rōshi is essentially living as a hermit in Gyokuryuji, he is still passionately committed to doing everything that he can to develop true men and true women—true people who can step beyond the world of rank, or separation, into this other consciousness, this other awareness. On 2nd July 2015, as we celebrate his 80th birthday with an exhibition of his artworks, I think it is very heartening that we have this particular artwork included (p98). The first character means "one" or "individual"; the rest means "no rank" and then "true person" or "human"— one true person with no rank (*ichi-mui no shinnin* as it is pronounced in Japanese).

Notice the way Shinzan Rōshi has brushed this calligraphy: the "one" is separated from the other characters. Anybody who has met Shinzan Rōshi will attest to his strength of character. He has been willing to stand alone for what he believes to be right and true every step of the way. In grounding yourself in this true-person place, the strength to stand up, the strength to at times even go against the current, is a very important aspect.

When we come together to practise, when we come together to meditate, we are letting go of position, of rank, of status, of any kind of comparison. We don't need any of that. When we let go of that level, we automatically and immediately enter this world of the true person of no rank. In this place we find strength, and this strength allows us to re-emerge and occupy our position or rank fully and truly, so that we can, within the individual details of our life, live out this truth.

A friend of mine who is very wise once told me, "Think globally and act locally." When we become aware of our global truth, we become able to act moment by moment from this fundamental connectedness, this fundamental adequacy. We don't have to earn it, we don't have to become in any way different to how we are. All we have to do, as Master Rinzai teaches us, is "look, look!" Allow your eyes to open! We are deeply blessed to have in Shinzan Rōshi a living example of how that can be.

© 大法
月 BAERNDAL

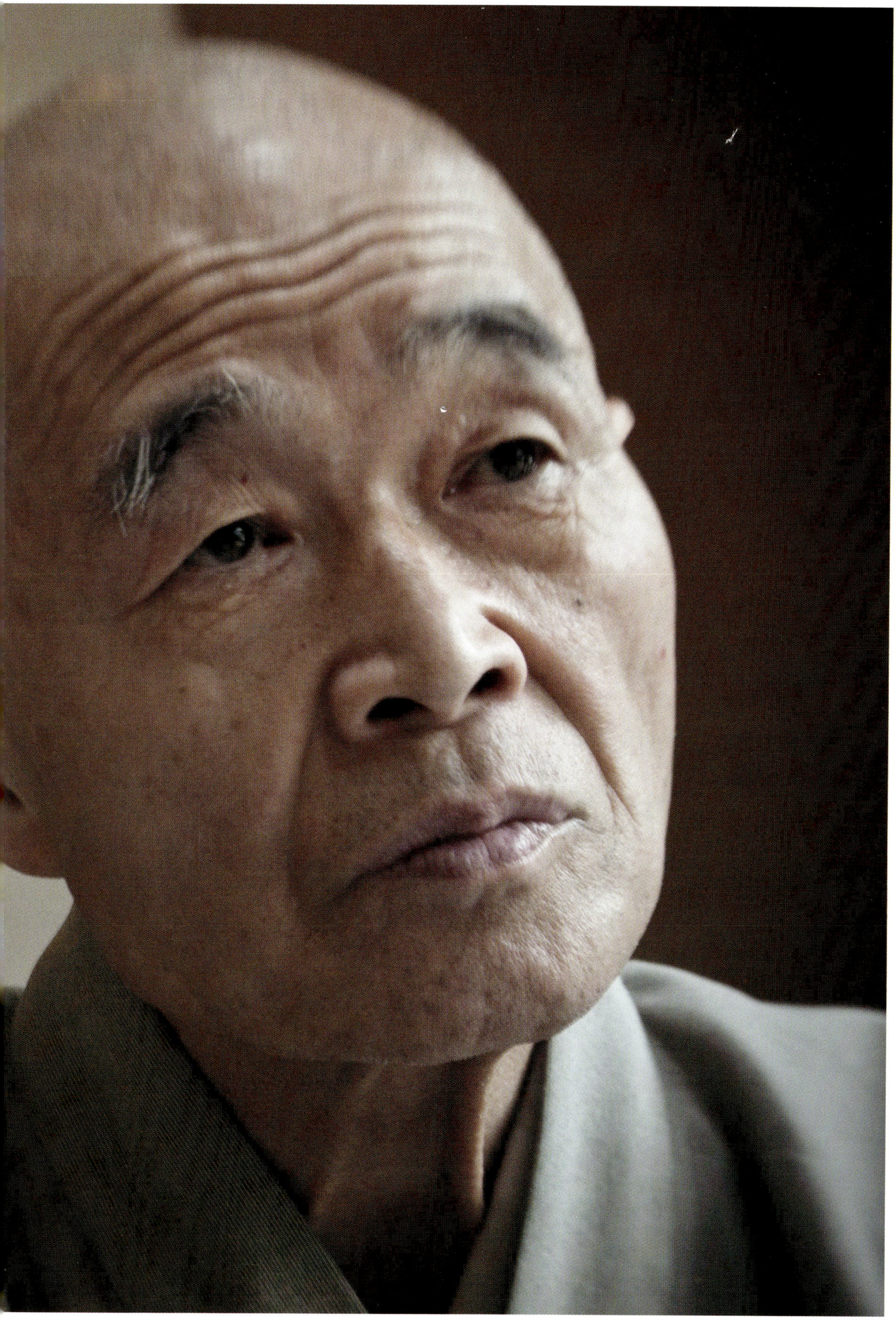

TALKS ON PRACTICE BY ZEN MASTER SHINZAN

Zen master Shinzan has been a very active teacher, both within Japan and the wider world. The following selections give a sampling of his practical oral teachings. He discusses a number of the *kōans* (spiritual questions) that form themes for meditation in the Rinzai approach to Zen, as well as the avowedly anti-*kōan* practice approach espoused by Rinzai master Bankei Yotoku, founder of Gyokuryuji, Shinzan Rōshi's temple. Pervading all is an insistence on the centrality of *kenshō*, the awakening process in Zen. Some of these talks were given in English, others in Japanese. Editing has been kept to a minimum in an attempt to accurately reflect Shinzan Rōshi's distinctive tone of voice.

How to Practise With a *Kōan*

From a talk at Gyokuryuji (2005)

First priority is *kenshō*! Second is *kenshō*! Third is *kenshō*! We say Rinzai Zen is *kōan* Zen. Not always true—Bankei Zenji is also Rinzai. A *kōan* is a story or case from the past. Usually in the past someone found enlightenment this way, so maybe you can right now. We call this enlightenment *kenshō*. *Kenshō* is to know your true self, your true nature. The word comes from an old verse from Daruma Daishi [Bodhidharma (5th or 6th century CE)], the first Zen teacher in China. His verse on Zen goes:

Kyōge betsuden
Furyu monji
Jikishin ninshin
Kenshō jōbutsu.

We can translate this as:

A special transmission outside the scriptures
Not relying on words and letters
Looking into the human heart
Knowing your true self, becoming Buddha.

When he went to teach the Emperor of China, the Emperor asked him, "Who is it that stands before me?" Daruma answered, "I don't know."

This is a very good question, maybe the first *kōan* in Zen—"Who are you?" Usually I give this as a first question before we begin other *kōans*, like in the West you have a starter before the meal. This is a starter *kōan*, "Who are you?"

So how do we practise? *Zazen* (sitting meditation) is very good. For many people it is difficult but it is important to try. The body is upright but relaxed. Hands in the lap. Eyes lowered or closed.

Breathing is important. In Japanese we say *hara* meaning the belly. When you do *zazen* it is good to breathe in your *hara*. When you breathe out, asking, "Who am I?" when you breathe in, looking, looking. Hakuin Zenji talks about *taigi*, meaning great doubt or questioning. He says it builds up like a ball in the *hara*, we make a ball of doubt, a ball of questioning, building, building every breath.

Zazen is important to start this but also we can practice *do-zen* [see calligraphy on p78]. *Zazen* is sitting-Zen; *do-zen* is moving-Zen. This *kōan* is very good for beginners because lifting the arm we can ask, "Who is lifting the arm?", turning the body we can ask, "Who is turning the body?"

In Zen, *samu* is also important. *Samu* means working meditation—working for everyone, helping not just me, me, me, but everyone. When we practise *samu*, we practise the *kōan*. During weeding time, we can ask "Who is weeding?", sweeping time "Who is sweeping?" Like this everything we do is the *kōan*. If you practise like this, even a little bit, soon the *kōan* is asking, the *kōan* is weeding, the *kōan* comes alive. Like this, *kenshō* will come.

In Zen a key phrase is *nari kiru*. *Nari kiru* means 100% become—when you drive a car, *nari kiru* to driving 100%; no gap. When eating, 100% eating. We cut-off all idle dualistic thinking. Then you can enjoy your life and get stronger in your practice. The best example I can give of *nari kiru* is when a farmer takes his spade to dig the soil and every time he digs his spade in, the *nari kiru* there is just movement—the soil is dug up. *Nari kiru* in movement is more effective to get *kenshō* than *nari kiru* in sitting. When we *nari kiru* to digging, we cut off our human attachment; when we pull weeds, we cut off attachment, so this is a very effective practice. This *nari kiru* is a treasure you can't compare with other treasures.

Unborn Zen

From a talk at Gyokuryuji (2006)

This temple, Gyokuryuji, was founded by Bankei Zenji (1622-1693). Now I am the teacher here. In Zen we say *garanbō*, meaning the "temple line" or "temple lineage". I am in the temple lineage of Bankei. He is my great-great-great something grandfather.

Bankei was a very important teacher but when he came here he was still a new teacher. He was looking for Zen master Gudo, the teacher of the emperor, to study with him, but Gudo was very busy and travelled much so Bankei didn't meet him. He ended up staying here instead. In his practice, Bankei was very severe—no eating, no sleeping, sitting, sitting.

But after his *kenshō* he was a very gentle teacher, very popular. I say Bankei Zen is the easy way. Hakuin Zen [after Zen master Hakuin (1686-1768)] now is more popular, but very difficult—hard training. Bankei is more soft. Hakuin is like the father and Bankei is like the mother. Two very great teachers. Later in his life, old Bankei came back here to lead a 90-day training retreat; 5000 people came. Can you imagine? This place is full with just 20 people! Maybe in Zen history he was the number one most popular teacher—a child can understand, a grandmother can understand. We say this place is where Bankei Zenji gave his first and last teaching. So we must remember him. These days in this temple we have people practising Bankei Zen and people practising Hakuin Zen together, side-by-side. Maybe the only place in Japan.

So what is Bankei Zen? Bankei Zen is "unborn Zen". Always in his teaching he says *fusho*, meaning unborn. What is this?

Zen means no life and no death. This is the path that we walk. Many things are born—thoughts are born and die, feelings are born and die, emotions are born and die. If we follow these born-and-die things we are not safe. Everything is changing. Like the ocean—waves rising and sinking, rising and sinking. If you say "This wave is good, I want; this wave is bad, I don't want," what happens? Nothing. Still the waves rising and sinking. This way in life we have no peace.

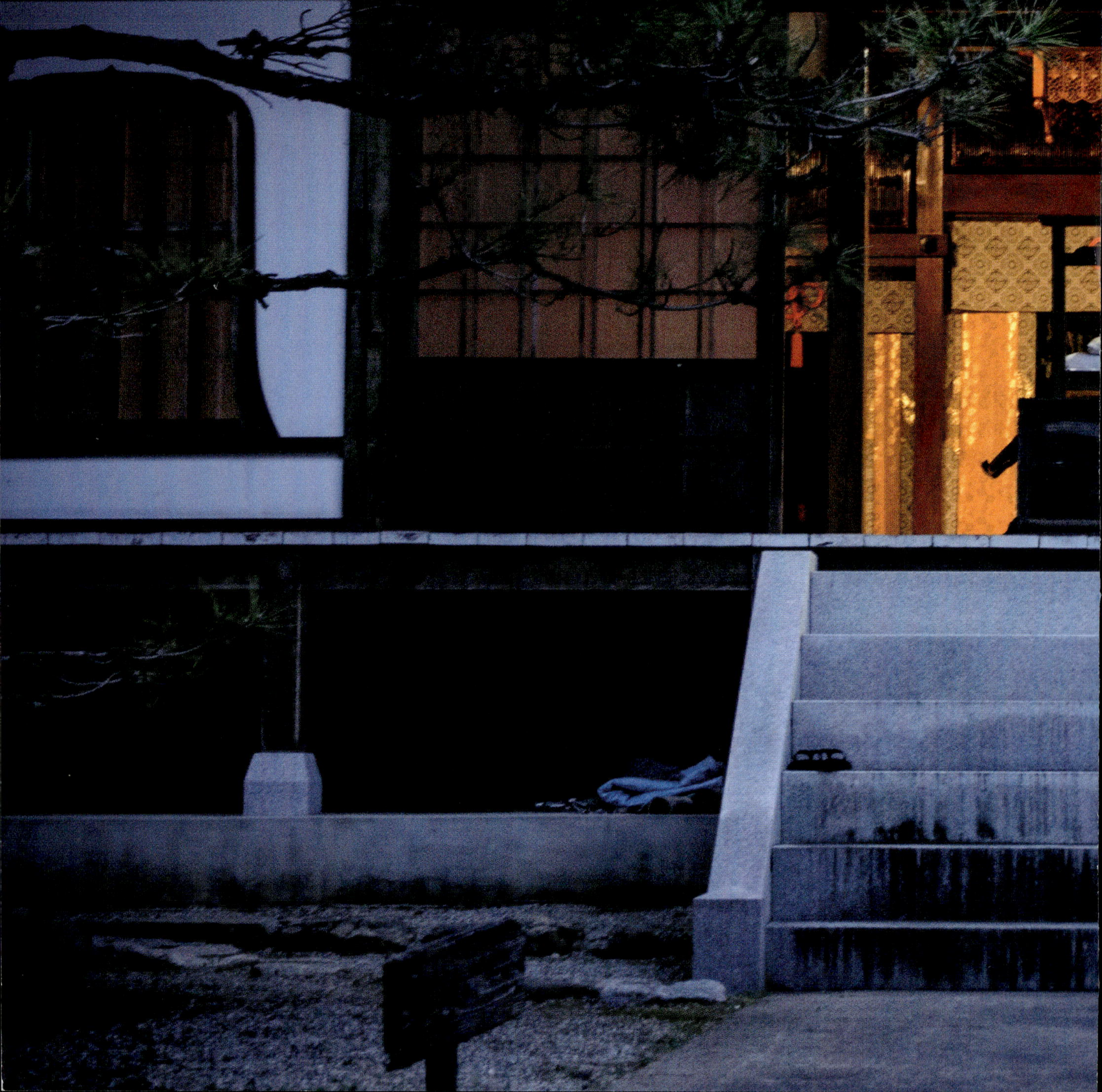

Gyokuryuji front steps at night

But the ocean, the whole ocean is always the same. No coming, no going. When you see the waves are just part of the ocean, you see everything is unborn. Everything is OK. You don't have to wait. Right now everything is like this. We can live like this—unborn sitting, unborn walking, unborn sleeping. Bankei says if you practise like this for 30 days then your whole life is different. You can be happy, peaceful. Everyone can do this.

Bankei also says, "Be like a mirror." A mirror just reflects everything. It doesn't choose. If a beautiful person walks by, it just reflects, and when they are gone, they are gone. No problem. If an ugly person walks by, it's the same. I recommend practising like Bankei Zenji. Then you have no problem. You can be happy.

The Practice of Mu

From a talk at Gyokuryuji at the start of a *sesshin* (Zen retreat) (May 2012)

Every day is a Zen training day but sometimes we have a big *sesshin* particularly focused on *kenshō*, enlightenment.

Each person usually thinks that his viewpoint is right, but from the perspective of Zen this is a mistake. Each one of us has an ego, so here in this hall we have 10 or 20 egos. In this world we have millions upon millions of self-centred viewpoints. Perhaps we have about seven billion people in the world but each with a different viewpoint.

But there is a time when this seven billion can become one. I expect that everyone here knows about this time of becoming one, but in case you don't, I can explain. As an example there is daytime and nighttime. Supposing everyone sleeps at the same time, isn't this sleep the same for everyone? In sleep time there is no opposition, no conflict.

This *sesshin* time is for us ordinary people to become enlightened persons or true people. All other sentient beings, like deer, frogs, birds, they all live naturally. Only humans go against nature and therefore damage nature and themselves. For many years we've been trying to find a nearby planet that might support life, but so far we find none that have the air and water suitable for human beings. At the same time we know that this planet is gradually becoming more contaminated. Eventually humans will not be able to live here. We've managed to send rockets to space and the moon, and this is a great achievement. But if we neglect the earth, life will become very difficult. We have been trying to conquer and change nature but this project has failed. Now we have to change ourselves, to find and follow the course of nature.

I believe that we make this change when we go from an ordinary person to an enlightened person. This has been done many times over the past two and a half thousand years. I really want you to get the enlightenment called *kenshō*.

In order to change or transform from an ordinary person to an enlightened person, we have to drop human wisdom. Of course human wisdom is useful and necessary for ordinary life. But for the purpose of *kenshō* we need Buddha's wisdom. I'm like a doctor of the human heart and from now I want you to pay close attention to what I say. The method I suggest to cure your suffering is over 800 years old.

In order to come here to the *zendō* (the meditation hall), you have to first come in through the gate. With this 800 year-old trusted technique, if you follow it diligently, you will enter the gate, you will get enlightenment.

Sometimes this gate is called in Zen "*mu mon*", the gate of *mu*. What is this *mu*?

A monk came to Zen master Jōshū (778–897 CE) and asked, "Does a dog have Buddha nature?"
Joshu answered, "*Mu.*"
This word means "no" or "not," but this negative is also positive.

When I was an *unsui* [novice monk] a new face in the monastery, one night on the mountain I shouted mu with my whole being and I was never the same again. I lost myself and experienced *kenshō*. How about you? Let's shout together,

"*Mu!*"

When we do this *mu* practice, we become one with the entire Universe. We become *mu*. We cut off our human idle thinking completely. One more time, OK?

"*Mu!*"

When we shout *mu*, some people can throw themselves into it fully, others not. Why? Perhaps because they suspect the technique and whether it genuinely works or not. And that's why their *mu* is not yet a real *mu*.

Entrust yourself to the technique as if you're the only person in the whole Universe, and the Universe becomes yourself. In this way you can develop a much more powerful *mu* and a strong energy of awakening.

It's just the same when you practise silently with *mu* in meditation. With this practice, half-hearted people bring their *mu* to *sanzen* [private Zen interview] and it can be rejected one year, two years, three years. But if you completely believe it, you can achieve *mu* during this *sesshin*. If you entrust yourself you can completely become *mu* right now.

So this *mu* is a sword which cuts off all our human wisdom. We have to completely cut off and throw it away and this *mu* will do that. We have evolved from monkeys to human beings, and now we have to evolve even further to awakened beings—that is our purpose.

This is urgent! Just imagine that you're about to fall down a cliff and you're calling for help. Nothing else is on your mind—that is the attitude you should adopt when you practice *mu* in shouting or in silence.

I ask you, when you call *mu* from the bottom of your heart, do you feel "like" or "dislike", "hot" or "cold?" Where do you feel these?

In the whole Universe I am the only one. This may be a little difficult to understand, but another way to consider this is when you practise *mu* you drop your separate ego. When you fully shout *mu* there are no dualistic feelings at all. You are the whole Universe.

The people who still hold back remain in separation. What I really want is for you, even for a split-second, to call *mu* and experience how it is when there is no human thinking.

In order to get the most benefit from this practice, *yaza* or night-sitting, is best. When you do this practice you get tired, and in this tiredness there is a time when there are no feelings at all, simply *mu*. When you fully practise *mu* the dualistic sense of ugly beautiful, good, bad is cut-off and you can enter the "*mu mon*" the gate of *mu*. Please practise with everything you've got.

The *Kōan* Practice of One Hand

Talk given in the meditation hall of Zen master Hakuin at Shoinji Temple, Shizuoka, Japan (May 2009)

We're sitting here together in Hakuin's *zendō*—the meditation hall of our great teacher. This is a special place to be and practise so I want to give you a present. Please listen to me carefully.

Master Hakuin asked, "You know the sound that two hands make [claps hands together]. Now what is the sound of one hand?" In this *zendō*, in Japan—in the world—many, many people have found enlightenment with this *kōan* from Hakuin. You can too.

Maybe this is the most famous *kōan*. Hakuin found it very, very effective. I often say to students, "Become only one hand in the whole Universe." What is this one hand sound? Asking deep inside. Doubt, doubt, doubt is very important.

You know normally we use two hands to make sound. Hakuin asks you to find the sound of one hand. So inside we ask, ask, ask, and when you pass through this asking, asking, it's so concentrated on this one side that you forget about the other side.

By this I mean cutting off all dualistic feelings. Both hands make a sound we can hear. That is dualistic. But what is the sound of one hand? When your hands are hit together it makes a sound but this *kōan* asks you to hear the sound of one hand. By pressing to hear the sound of one hand, that creates questioning, and the questioning gets bigger and bigger and this ask, ask, ask, fills the whole Universe. In the process of pursuing this why, why, why, we cut off everything and when we go to *sanzen*, roshi says, "In the entire Universe only one hand." What is the meaning? Ask, ask, ask—this doubt or questioning is so important. In that time not just a small doubt but a great doubt is important—it cuts off all dualistic feelings.

During the practice we may get something called *ma-kyo* (or sometimes *shokyo*), meaning imaginations, visions or delusions. But forget about these. What we are seeking is an emptying—even for one second. Why? Because once I cut off human ideas, everyone becomes oneness.

The dualistic world is full of confrontations—confrontations of countries, of religions, of husband and wife; always confrontations. This practice should not be just another religion among many. You have to go beyond religion with your Zen practice. If religion remains it's difficult to accept other religions.

The most important thing is called in Japanese, *nari kiru*. This means completely losing yourself where there is no dualistic idea or feeling. One second by one second—cut-off, cut-off. When we become one with the entire Universe, everything you've accumulated is gone. We have accumulated human wisdom, knowledge, experience. It's difficult to cut-off, but when we throw ourselves into asking, asking, we become very close to how a baby is. Human wisdom tends to come from the head rather than the *hara* [abdomen] but if you keep asking in the *hara* and keep practising it, you'll surely achieve *kenshō*. Hakuin liked to talk about a man from the next village who got *kenshō* in two days. Maybe you can do it right now sitting in this famous *zendō*. But it is not necessary to hurry or rush. If your asking, asking is continuous, you'll surely get *kenshō*. Please practise well.

Your Original Face

From a talk at Gyokuryuji (May 2009)

"What is your original face before your parents were born?" This has become an important beginners *kōan* in our system.

We come from the Mino branch of the Inzan line of *kōan* study. Mino is this area [around Gyokuryuji]—this land of mountains and rivers. Many famous Rinzai people come from the city, like Kyoto or Kamakura. We are in the country so things are a little bit different. Inzan (1751-1814) is an important teacher in our line. He was the founder of my first *sōdō* (training monastery), Zuiryoji, in Gifu City, maybe 25 kilometres from here. So Zen master Inzan was in this area and he was a very strong teacher (maybe a little bit rough though!). He re-organised all the *kōans* into one system, so for us he is an important teacher.

And Inzan Rōshi decided this "orginal face" *kōan* was important so we study it. Now, together, I want everybody in this temple to study this *kōan*. If you pass this original face *kōan*, you can be called a true Zen person.

We can study together with "group *sanzen*". What is this? Firstly look at the opposite. In modern Zen, students go one-by-one to the teacher for a private interview. This is called *sanzen*. It is good, but sometimes very slow. When I studied the ancient Zen texts from the T'ang Dynasty in China, the so-called "Golden Age" of Zen, I found that most Zen study was in a group.

Of course advanced practice might be solitary. This temple was the hermitage of Zen master Bankei. Just across the river, Zen master Kanzan (1227-1360) practised alone as a cowman for eight years. Now I practise here mostly alone. Solitary practice is very good. But a new-face [beginner] usually needs a group. People practising together is very powerful. So here at Gyokuryuji I decided to keep one-to-one interviews but also to restore the ancient Zen practice of group *sanzen*.

There are different ways of Zen study with a group. Sometimes I ask each person in turn the same *kōan* and they answer in public. From my response the next person learns something and together we refine our understanding. Sometimes I question just one person deeper and deeper, and everyone listens, and we all learn. Sometimes the student asks me. With group *sanzen* we can be very flexible. Daizan Rōshi showed me a way of group *sanzen* with a student facing a student that is very good. This [original face] *kōan* shows the power of this face-to-face meeting. Do you know the story?

Daikan Enō (638-713 CE) was an illiterate woodcutter living in the south of China looking after his old mother. He had no education, no practice—except maybe natural practice or natural meditation in the mountains cutting wood. One day he was carrying down a load of wood and he heard a monk chanting the Diamond Sutra. Boom! He had a big *kenshō*, big enlightenment.

People said, "You should go to the fifth ancestor [Kōnin (601–674 CE)] to study." So Enō walked thirty days north to the fifth ancestor's temple. In those days south Chinese people were low-status so this woodcutter, with no training and no education, was of the lowest status. But Konin could see—when meeting him, he said "Yes, nice person, nice understanding."

He gave Enō work in the kitchen—moving Zen—and the fifth ancestor watched him, checking his mindstate. After a time he decided, "Yes Enō is good, he should be my successor." He called him to his room at midnight while everyone was sleeping and gave him Dharma transmission and a special robe—the robe of Daruma [Bodhidharma], the first ancestor. Inside the robe were written true words, Dharma words, like a certificate. I gave the same to Daizan Rōshi when he became my successor.

In the temple many monks wanted this robe, this transmission, so Enō had to escape. And when they found out they were very angry. "This person is not a monk, he can't read—this is impossible. We must chase him, get the robe back." So they did, chasing, chasing him into the mountains.

A monk called Myō who was very strong (ex-military) caught up with Enō. Enō left the robe on a rock and when Myo came and saw the robe Enō said, "Do you want the robe or the Dharma?"

Gyokuryuji

Shinzan Rōshi with Alex Horikitsune Reinke

Myō said, "Really, I want the Dharma."

Enō said, "Not thinking good, not thinking evil, what is your original face before your parents were born?" Original face means true nature—what are you really?

Myō was looking, looking; Enō facing him. They were together how long I don't know. "What is my true face?"—looking, looking. Then Myō exclaimed "I got it! It is the same as somebody drinking water—they know directly whether it is hot or cold." No thinking, no learning, they just know. This is *kenshō*.

You people here are not monks. We say in Zen, "new-face"—a new person. Maybe you haven't studied sutras (Buddhist texts), and maybe you come from far away. Maybe you're a little bit like Enō. You can find your original face, your true nature. Original face-to-original face, asking each other the question and looking, like Myō and Enō. Soon Myō found his true nature, soon you will too. Please find quickly. You will be very happy and I will be very happy—and the world needs happy, awake people. Your practice is important.

Zen Philosophy – Nishida Kitaro

Part of a talk "A Zen Model of Human Development" at the Oxford University Centre for Buddhist Studies (June 2011)

Nishida Kitaro (1870-1945) is important for us because he tried to put forward a philosophical interpretation of Zen. In his diary he wrote, "It would be good if after achieving *satori* [enlightenment] in one great truth, one could explain it to others in a modern theory." This was his work. He studied western and eastern philosophy so he could be a bridge between the East and the West. He is the most important philosopher of the "*Kyoto Gakuha*" , the Kyoto school of philosophy. Many of you here are involved in work where thinking is your job. I think Nishida can help you.

In his life he experienced much suffering. His brother died, his wife died, his children died—much, much suffering. At age 14 his maths teacher introduced him to Zen. Later he practised in many temples and with many roshis. The first temple he studied at was Engakuji in Kamakura while he was studying at Tokyo University. He started to practise with the *mu kōan*.

We study this *mu*, what is *mu*? Looking, looking in meditation. Nishida in his diary writes "Every day *zazen* practice—morning, afternoon, evening." He was a sincere student. What is *mu*? Looking, looking. This was his first job. With the practice of *mu* we say *nari kiru*, meaning "become *mu*." *Nari kiru* also means cut-off—cut-off idle thinking. Only one *mu* in the whole Universe. But *nari kiru* is also "when washing dishes, only washing dishes"; "when thinking, only thinking". Yes we can *nari kiru* thinking! Thinking-time is 100% thinking. Listening-time is 100% listening.

Many years Nishida practised like this—many teachers, much reading, much thinking, *nari kiru* everything. Then—*kenshō*, enlightenment. In his diary he wrote, "REBIRTH... awakened from a bad dream. From a rotten tree somehow a new bud can sprout. Today I was most happy."

His job was then to explain. We say "*Nishida tetsugaku*", meaning "Nishida philosophy". Western ideas and Eastern ideas explaining Zen enlightenment for modern people. He had read Kant, Hegel, Bergson, and wrote about *junsui keiken* or "pure experience". Nishida defines this pure experience as direct experience without idle thinking. In the university world, Nishida created a new unique philosophy that provided a Western philosophical framework for Zen experience.

Also he wrote about *jikaku*, meaning "self-awakening." Everywhere people are trapped. He called this self-awakening the state of "absolute free will." University people, you are very important. The world needs you to experience *jikaku* and lead the world with new understanding. Please practise like the example of Nishida.

Buddha's Enlightenment Anniversary Talk

Talk at the London Buddha Jayanthi festival, 2600th anniversary of the Buddha's enlightenment, (29th May 2011). Organised by the London Buddhist Vihara with help from the Buddhist Society.

Good afternoon everybody. In commemoration of the 2600th anniversary of the Buddha's enlightenment, I'd like to talk from the viewpoint of Shakyamuni himself about his training. He said, "In the entire Universe I am alone, only one."

Following this teaching, in my own life I trained very hard. This "only one" is not such a very difficult thing to achieve, it's possible for everybody to achieve this.

What it means is sit alone, by oneself, until you come to understand that there's a moment when our thinking activity stops. At that time, we realise, "In the entire world, I am only one." When this happens our old human knowledge has disappeared. We should realise that this "one" is inherent in all of us. We all should realise that this is what the Buddha himself realised. In this time, this moment, our human likes, dislikes and all the rest of duality disappears.

A baby is just like this. But when we grow up we accumulate information and develop "human wisdom". But if we manage to get rid of this desire, this human information, we reach a stage where there are no dualities at all—no likes, dislikes, no big, no small. Nothing is a problem. In this moment we should deeply recognise, "Yes, this is the enlightenment that Buddha realised." In memory of the Buddha's enlightenment 2600 years ago, we should all recognise this.

If we look at the present time, people are fighting each other and polluting the earth. These problems do not stop because we only use our human knowledge. We have to have two wisdoms—one is human-based wisdom [human knowledge], the other one is the wisdom of Buddha.

Buddha's wisdom is found through cutting-off all dualities. On this very happy day we should realise that Buddha is our kind father. After 2600 years, human beings have still not realised this, but I hope the human beings in this room can realise these two wisdoms. What I have been saying is in accordance with Buddhist doctrine which I will explain now.

In the Heart Sutra it speaks of "*hannya* wisdom". This is another phrase for Buddha's wisdom. With this non-dual wisdom we experience that everything has no existence or solidity. Even the Universe itself is not solid but temporary. Everything is moving and changing. There is no permanent existence.

The second wisdom is called *yugagyo* or *yogacara* [literally yoga practice]. It shows that reality (everything) is created by the human heart. There are hundreds of people in this room and everyone has a different viewpoint. Everyone is convinced "I am right." This is a mistake and a source of suffering. We should experience and realise Buddha's teachings in these two areas, and, by using them, contribute to society. By stressing the importance of following Buddha's teachings I conclude this talk. Thank you.

木法
月 BAERNDAL

ENCOUNTERS WITH SHINZAN RŌSHI

Daizan Rōshi remembers his first week at Gyokuryuji

Week One at Gyokuryuji

It was the beginning of April, the time when most Zen temples in Japan have an elaborate ceremony to mark the anniversary of the Buddha's birth. Instead, our Zen master, Shinzan Rōshi, had us out in the bamboo grove below Gyokuryuji Temple digging up fresh bamboo shoots to eat. The ease and vigour of his movements belied his seventy-odd years. Bamboo roots are tough and awkward to dig so after a few hours work we rested in the shade drinking *mugi cha*, chilled barley tea.

Shinzan Rōshi sat beside me. "No ceremony today," he said. " We make new baby Buddha like this." He made digging movements with his hands.

I was new in the temple having spent fourteen years practising in a formal and tradition-minded Zen monastery in the UK. Shinzan Rōshi's freewheeling style and palpable joy were very different.

"Baby is very beautiful," he continued. "Human baby is just completely perfect. When hungry it cries, when sleepy it sleeps." He smiled and added, "Perhaps in Christian Bible, The Garden of Eden is like this baby time. But it is a very, very short time. We grow, study, leave the happy garden and long, long time, maybe longest of any animal, we grow.

"As we grow, grow, grow, the me, me, me is stronger and stronger. This is me," he pointed to himself. "That is world," he pointed away.

"Adult time is split. Little me: great big world. This is needed. Adult person is responsible so I must know myself, take charge of my life. I wanted to be big businessman, make money, build something." He laughed. I had heard previously that his business ventures had been spectacular disasters.

"But also adult time is very lonely. Little me: great big world. That is why we practise." He stood up. "Our practice is to now dig bamboo."

Over the following months and years, I watched Shinzan Rōshi expand on these simple truths. Whoever came with a wish to learn, he would meet them where they were. I saw farmers, gangsters, stressed executives, people of all types coming to the temple.

He welcomed them all, seeming to take particular delight in those who'd been treated most harshly by life. Frequently, people would come who were so damaged that their behaviour would disrupt temple routine. The rest of us trainees had to learn how to manage the situation to benefit all concerned. Believing that "the lotus blooms in the heart of the fire," Shinzan Rōshi would constantly create situations where the *kōan* of daily life was unavoidable.

He was also delighted by those who came with a burning desire to find the truth. He gave a Dharma talk every morning, frequently starting with "First priority is *kenshō*; second priority is *kenshō*; third priority is *kenshō*." Noting my previous background, Shinzan Rōshi took great amusement in un-stuffing me from monastic formalities. My practice with him was intense and stretching. We lived through fire, human drama and physical exposure. Looking back I feel tremendously blessed.

One *mu* in the whole Universe

"This is not your training place." Shinzan Rōshi points towards the forested mountain behind the temple. "That is your training place."

Since I arrived at this Rinzai Zen temple in central Japan, he's repeatedly told me to find "only one *mu* in the whole universe." He's talked about how in his own training he'd spent fourteen months plunging himself into *mu*, trying to find the meaning of it, the reality behind the classic interchange from a thousand years ago:

A monk asked Master Jōshū, "Does a dog have the Buddha Nature?" Jōshū responded "*Mu*." Not yes, not no, but "*mu*."

One day the young monk, Shinzan shouted "*MU*!!!" putting all his life into it, everything; just gave it all away, and immediately experienced *kenshō*, a taste of enlightenment. Now, again, he's sending me back up the mountain to do the same work, to throw everything away, shouting into the night. As he speaks he's totally focused, completely present. It's clear he believes I can do it. The first time I came to *sanzen* [private interview] with an answer, my *mu* was a bleat, a little, feeble nothing, "It's not so easy to find *mu*," he said, "*Kufu, kufu*." So now, after fourteen years of Sōtō Zen monastery training; *zazen, zazen, zazen*, descending deeper and deeper into stillness, all of that work has to go on one side. This master has little time for endless hours of sitting. Zen is action or it is nothing. We spend much of the day working, "*Kufu, kufu*;" grinding away on our *kōans*. And then comes the night.

Darkness comes quickly at this little temple surrounded by small, steep mountains. Bamboos and dense tree cover wrap around the timbered buildings and gravel gardens. About 400 years ago this piece of land was levelled in an earthquake. The early days are connected with the great Zen master Bankei Yotaku. After each of his great realisations he retired to a little hermitage here to mature his experience. Later he developed the buildings, giving them the name Gyokuryuji—Dragon Jewel Temple—and later held a practice period here teaching 5,000 people. Once Zen master Bankei wrote:

"Die then live
Day and night with the world
Once you have done this, then you can
Hold the world right in your hand."

As the light falls, his life-size wooden statue, glowering behind its peeling paint in the Founder's Hall, would be almost invisible. Even out here on the mountainside, it's getting hard to see. The path faded to nothing well below me. As I pull my way up though the trees, monkeys crash above in the canopy. I'm starting to pant and leaf mould odours fill my nose. Suddenly I hit the top. There's no view, the tree cover's too dense, but up above the stars are breaking through.

I climb down a little onto the reverse side of the mountain, so my noise won't disturb the temple. I begin to shout. "*MU, MU, MU*," throwing my life energy into each call, extending the, "*u-u-u-u-u*." At first my voice is weedy and thin but, breath by breath, it gathers strength. One by one, then in crowds, come the resistances, "You can't do this. You'll wreck your voice. Your living is based on your voice. You'll get reported for disturbing the peace and deported from Japan! You'll fall and break a leg up here and no one will find you, and anyway you've got no health insurance. And then deeper stuff, fear, fear, fear. Terror of complete destitution on every level. Ancient memories from our collective past of others who found something real and got persecuted for it. Anger over teachers who held out false promises and led me up blind alleys. My body begins to tremble and then convulse. As I shout, I feel like a chimney belching toxic smoke into the night.

As the smoke releases breath by breath, I feel my voice open and deepen, I suck in huge lungfuls of the night and catapult it back. The process builds its own momentum, taking on a whole new realm of urgency. So "*MU-U-U-U, M-U-U-U-U-U*."

Every morning after sutra-chanting, Shinzan Rōshi fills the Dharma Hall with incandescent vigour as he teaches the Rinzai Roku, the ninth-century founding document of this school.

"Followers of the way, you must throw away everything. Kill the Buddha, kill the ancestors.
In the hall, the master took the high seat. He said: "On your red flesh body there is a true man of no rank who is always going in and out of the face of each one of you. Those who have not yet confirmed him, look, look!"

Shinzan Rōshi focused his teaching differently. Rather than preparing priests to go out and continue the family business (as would happen in most temples), he emphasises the importance of developing a true understanding. I throw myself into it. "MU-U-U-U, MU-U-U-U-U,"

As my voice fails, I sit in silence, going deeper and deeper into *mu*. After a while, tiredness takes over and my concentration fades. I begin to lose body heat and come back to awareness. So I sit on this mountain-top suspended between exhaustion and cold.

After a bit my voice comes back and I stand up and begin to bellow again, waking echoes from the opposite slopes. And on it goes all night, alternating sitting and shouting, sitting and shouting. I'm numb with tiredness. A memory that someone once told me you can last longer without food than you can without sleep crawls across my brain. But anyway, as the sky turns to grey, I'm still here. There's no way I'd have found my way down the trackless slopes without a little light to see my way. So now I stumble and slide down through the trees, down to morning sutra chanting, sprinting through the texts in an accelerating drone. Rōshi lectures again on the Rinzai Roku:

"Cast away all idle thinking."

His voice and energy keep my spine from sagging. Then it's time for *zazen*, more *mu, mu, mu*. As I go into *sanzen* and bow, I'm just too tired for anything.

"Well?" he looks at me appraisingly. "Show me only one *mu* in the whole Universe."

A roar erupts out of me, through me, through everything. I blink in surprise. He laughs. "Ninety percent."

184

185

Gyokuryuji nestled in the mountains surrounded by bamboo forests

Matt Shinkai Kane

Weeding in the wrong place

The first time I met Shinzan Rōshi he was driving up the steep driveway into Gyokuryuji in a big shiny dark blue Toyota Crown Royal and leaned out the window to ask what the hell I was doing weeding his irises. He wasn't very happy but seemed pretty relaxed for someone who had just lost about half their crop. What was I doing? Later he invited me up to his living quarters (in the building before the fire) and asked if I had any questions about Zen. I remember sitting on a cushy green couch feeling like I was in the middle of a tornado, the encounter oscillating from him shouting at his assistant, to incredibly simple answers about Zen practice with, all the while, the resident chihuahua attacking my legs. It was quite a situation and the energy he and the room held was electric. When I slunk back down to my room hours later I knew I had stumbled upon something special and it was hard to sleep that night.

This first encounter with Shinzan Rōshi came during the second year of my English teaching job in central Japan. Life was so-so at the time. However, it was indeed true for me, as well as for others I've met, that once you've crossed paths with that kind of a being—one who has so clearly seen through life, death, and everything else—it's difficult to continue doing what you've been doing up to that point. It's difficult to continue living the same way pretending that that kind of person doesn't exist.

Matt Shinkai went on to study with Shinzan Rōshi at Gyokuryuji for another five years.

Simply another situation to meet head on

Shinzan Rōshi had no qualms about letting anybody come stay and practise at Gyokuryu-ji. His temple was listed in the "mental health healing places" guide of Japan and open to people regardless of their diagnosis or problems. He allowed people with bi-polar disorder, schizophrenia, depression—nothing was off limits—to stay and live alongside his Zen students. This was considered practice in its highest form. He refused to turn anybody away and did his very best to give each person what he or she needed to improve. Needless to say, the police were called on more than one occasion.

Once there was a particularly difficult case of a man named Nagata-san who had a sweet side and an ugly, furious side too. Rōshi always stood up for Nagata-san even though his personality was uncontrollable and explosive. He had a wooden samurai sword that he used to attack his walls and bed with, and to threaten others. One day he let the dogs into the hen house. Once, when Shinzan Rōshi was away, Nagata-san rode his bike down to the village and was screaming at the top of his lungs just for good fun. The police were called and, after two additional incidents, Nagata-san was taken away to a mental health clinic. Shinzan Rōshi would visit him every month. That was a difficult, scary time to be at the temple but we could never complain about it, we were expected to bear it and learn from it. I have to admit that I was relieved once Nagata-san left, but to Shinzan Rōshi it was always simply another situation to meet head on.

Today, out in Oregon, as we slowly start our new Zen community (Matt now lives in Eugene, Oregon, USA) I try to remember to be like Shinzan Rōshi. Sometimes hurt, traumatised, difficult people come through the door and are scary to work with. I try to do my best to remember how he never turned anyone away and would pour himself into truly meeting each person. Some people it didn't really work for, some people it did, but he never stopped trying and never gave up on anybody. I know of very few people who possess this kind of fearless open heartedness to do what Shinzan Rōshi did day-in and day-out for decades; I know of very few people who have seen through the dualistic mind so thoroughly to be uncompromising in this area—to see each being's inherent goodness so clearly. It feels like a rare gift to have crossed paths with a person who can do that.

Matt Shinkai Kane with Shinzan Rōshi in 2006

The garden at Gyokuryuji

David Bernstein

I was fortunate to go on *sesshin* (retreat) with Daizan Rōshi to Gyokuryuji in 2009. Shinzan Rōshi made an immediate impression. Through the brilliance of his teaching, Shinzan Rōshi was able to take complex Zen concepts, distil them down and make them personally relevant to everyone in the room. I learnt a great deal during the two weeks I spent at his temple.

I was also struck by how effortlessly Shinzan Rōshi could embody any particular role. At the beginning of the retreat I was working in the temple garden, when I was approached by an old man in gardening clothes. He patiently explained to me how I could use the trowel I was using to pull weeds out of the ground. I assumed he was a temple groundsman. Then it dawned on me—I'd been talking to Shinzan Rōshi himself!

Shinzan Rōshi took on another guise in the *sanzen* room. He would be direct, to the point, and quite fearsome. More than one person on the retreat compared him to a samurai warrior. When it was time for us to have *sanzen*, we would all line up with some degree of trepidation! But on other occasions he would be chatty and relaxed. And when we had to get up early one morning to go to Kyoto, he came out to see us and waved us off with a smile on his face. One of the other retreat participants who was sitting next to me on the bus said that he felt like he'd been seen off by his kind grandfather.

In both his words and actions, Shinzan Rōshi was able to fully embody Zen practice. He left a very strong impression on me.

Mark Westmoquette

I first met Shinzan Rōshi when I went over to Japan with Daizan Rōshi for *sesshin* (retreat) in 2010. Shinzan's Rōshi was unlike anyone I'd ever met before. Physically he looked like what you might expect of any 76 year old (as he was at the time)—thin, short, slightly stooped and wrinkled. But there was something about him that immediately struck me. He was the embodiment of grounded strength—power, but in wonderfully gentle, warm way. His presence as he walked into a room was tangible.

Having never been to Japan before, and having never been to a temple or done a Zen retreat, I was slightly overwhelmed by everything, so my memory is a little hazy. In the first couple of days of the retreat I remember him introducing us to a couple of famous *kōans*, but his English was at times hard to decipher and we regularly had to ask Daizan Rōshi for a summary. From the very start, though, he implored us to strive toward oneness. In our meditation, become one with the *kōan*; when eating, become one with the food; when weeding the garden, become one with the action of pulling up the weed. Shinzan's term for this is "*nari kiru*" (literally to become cut off).

There was no messing about. Driven by this incredibly strong, deeply rooted but utterly unattached, unquestionably wise Zen master, I dove into the practice and applied myself as hard as I could. Sitting, walking, sitting, stretching, weeding, eating, sitting, sipping tea, sleeping, I tried to *nari kiru* everything I was doing.

On this retreat, Shinzan Rōshi had decided not to do formal *sanzen*, so if we wanted a chat he would encourage us to just get up from wherever we were and come and find him. He'd often be up in his study, out in the garden, or taking care of his dogs. After a couple of days of hard slog, discomfort, and restlessness, I settled in to the practice, and in the afternoon of day four something shifted. I had about three hours where I completely disappeared. I was doing the sitting and walking but there was no me doing it! At some point I realised what had happened and went, feeling a bit dazed and confused to Daizan Rōshi. He told me to go and find Shinzan Rōshi.

After searching all over the temple I eventually found

him far up the bank with his work clothes and gloves on, clearing bamboo. I managed to clamber up to a clearing in the weeds about 10 metres from where he was and told him what I'd experienced. "Ahh" he called out, "you are now zen-man. From an ordinary hu-man you are now zen-man!" One of the *kōans* he'd been describing to us during the retreat was "Basho's Stick", which points you towards realising that there's nothing holy in this world. I think this situation was another example of an answer—I was describing my first experience of Zen awakening while half way up a bank surrounded by weeds shouting up to the master covered in sweat and brambles! Nothing sacred there!

I've had the fortune now to be able to attend three five-day *sesshins* led by Shinzan Rōshi, and he remains the most incredible person I've ever met. The power, strength, solidity and vigour of his being absolutely blows you away. And he has this almost baby-like warmth, curiosity and contentedness that goes along with his smile of 100% acceptance and an infectiously playful laugh. When we were in Japan on retreat last July, I had the honour of filming Daizan Rōshi interviewing Shinzan about his life and how he got into Zen. He tells quite a story [see Chapter 5 of this book].

Filming Daizan Rōshi interviewing Shinzan Rōshi just after our sesshin retreat in July 2014.

Dainei Tracy

I met Shinzan Rōshi the first time in the *sanzen* room on retreat in 2011 at Gaunts House in Dorset.
He had set us all the *mu kōan* and I didn't know what we were supposed to be doing with it at all, although I heard someone shout it out as a sort of power sound when it was their turn with him.

I felt completely green with very little direct experience, which I thought I ought to try to explain to Shinzan, all the while hoping I wasn't wasting his time. He sat rooted in full beautiful Zenji-reality with an energy field that I hadn't ever expected to get so close to in real life. In contrast I was paralysed and idiotic, which was great as I was raw. It did not feel so great though...

He asked me to just try, try, and I mewed (strangled cat), so self conscious and tangled up... definitely not any sort of unified *MU*—nowhere near close.

He shook his head, no..no...no... I cried a little.

I was ashamed and wondered how I had got myself into this embarrassing situation where I was so obviously out of my depth (yet all the while knowing this is what I had been waiting for!).

Gathering myself up, I said sorry, and that the trouble is that I had no confidence, not realising until I said it how true it was, and pretty sure he would ask me to leave, as obviously I had made a mistake thinking I could just jump in with no previous form...
He smiled a brilliant smile just then, and told me he could help me with that...
What??? I couldn't believe my luck.
And help he did.

The way that he is, and this process of finding the

Shinzan Rōshi with his birthday cake, July 2014

point of ones own unified energy, "only One *mu* in the whole Universe!", as he encouraged us all, gave me an absolute unmistakable mirror.
Shinzan graciously accepted all efforts—sometimes he was a direct reflection, sometimes he held the Rōshi ground while floundering took place. He looked like an inscrutable visitation from ancient Japan one day with a fan, another day a sword or paper, which he used to illustrate duality and impermanence... Strangely, I found myself dreaming a vision of that day's fan or paper when I woke each morning. I felt somehow tel-

epathically connected and absorbed.

In the centre of it all somewhere he showed me the place between my mind and big fat nothing, in my memory it is as though we were nose to nose and standing up, hovering even, but I know we were always seated on the ground across from each other.

He said, "Not Being" and my mind was caught like a fish, being, being; and then he said, "Not Nothing" and that statement completely erased all the suicidal nihilism that I had been trapped in since childhood.
It all shifted, gone, no mind.
It broke the back of my identification with the workings of my mind and set me on a freedom journey. Shinzan Rōshi is humorous, kind and classically stern and vulnerable with that beautiful, compact feeling, energy of Zen discipline, the total mindfulness of "nari kiru."

Nari kiru, he said, is the only way to live 'no mind' (this was when I asked him again last year). It is becoming totally one with any doing that needs to be done, cutting all else away as soon as we realise we are hooked or distracted, again and again. He is a master and I am amazed at my luck that I have met him and been able to spend time with him.

With Shinzan Rōshi the mystery of self becomes concentrated and exposed, anything extra is shed quickly, and then he kindly reflects back to you "you are a Zen woman" and "you are a Zen teacher".

Eventually on the fourth day my *MU* got an eighty-five percent from him.
Result!

He helped me find my guts, now I know how to digest experience as it comes and goes, gaining a little more confidence step by step as time goes by.

Nectar for the soul straight from the Zen Character himself!

Chris Owen

Picture the scene. A week's trip to the central mountains of Gifu, Japan to our home temple in Gyokuryuji including a five day *sesshin*. Up early with each day filled with silence and meditation. Day 3. My alarm rings at 4.25am. Time for a quick shower before early morning *taiso* (Zen exercise). I stumble in the darkness out of bed into my *samu* (informal work/meditation clothes). Towel in hand. The sliding doors open on to the outside balcony. I go across the balcony, open the door into the kitchen, down the stairs to the shower. Watch your head on the low ceiling—lost in the early morning blackness. I'm in the kitchen now, shoes off anticipating the early morning wake up bell.

Now the shower is just down the stairs. I reach towards the railing. A startled cry. My cry. There in the shadows a silhouette, robed darkness. I leap back, eyes desperately trying to get accustomed to the dark. And there before me Shinzan Rōshi in his finest robes ready for the early morning. He stands there looking straight at me. I murmur some sort of apology. "A Zen priest does not make such noise" he says. And with that he is gone. Leaving me in the shocked darkness.

Chris leading the chanting on *sesshin* at Gyokuryuji, July 2014

An explosive moment, ripping aside all that noise and energy—into the stillness, the emptiness of that moment in the pre-dawn kitchen. For a moment everything had gone—the steps downstairs, the shower, the anticipated bell, the rigours of the day ahead. Just the infiniteness of that moment. And an overwhelming sense of the rawness of the present.

I'm back in London now. Back to the day job. Bouncing along in the noise and busyness of the day. But somewhere amongst all that doing, the sense of a robed figure deeply grounded in the present moment bringing me abruptly back into the here and now.

Ed Evans

It was the summer of last year (2014) and I was half way through the second day of my first proper Zen *sesshin*. I was waiting in line to see Shinzan privately for an interview which would test my understanding, and I can't overstate how highly I was valuing this. We weren't going to have many chances to see him and I knew what was on offer with Zen and had been wearing my zeal like a badge of pride. He was going to know how serious I was, like full-on *ninja* serious, I was going to make sure, and then he would be all "Ahhh, you are true warrior!" and impart the Secrets Of The Universe to me.

I walked in, barely sat down, and he dismissed me from the room.

I'd actually met Shinzan before about a year prior. He came down to London and I followed him back to where he was staying. I garbled a question to him about Zen and then proceeded to completely miss his detailed response because I was too busy scrutinising him for greatness. (I later reflected this isn't a kind thing to do when meeting a person.) He didn't seem particularly great. He didn't even look particularly happy. He seemed like a perfectly ordinary elderly Japanese gentleman who was perturbed that some punk kid like myself was bugging him.

Writing this now, even though I want to say that he is actually perfectly ordinary, because that would be such a Zen thing to say, he completely isn't.

I mean, sure, he's a human being, and all human beings are unique and such, and he expresses moods like you and I do instead of floating along in some beatific haze all the time, but there's something else that is scarcely identifiable but utterly palpable which I'm going to try and articulate.

Firstly it started to become clear that there was simply no neuroses about his humanness. He could be whatever—angry, sad, whatever. Then I started to notice how every time he was one of these things, it was so complete, so fully committed to, that it seemed to leave no taste upon the world, it just burnt out utterly as it was happening. Actually his whole being is like this, down to the smallest gesture. The effect is one that brings your anxieties to the surface only to have them blown away as utterly non applicable. He is, literally, a "force of nature", and kind of amusing when he's comforting and sympathetic to your problems in his words because every cell of his body sends the message that there are no such things as problems.

In Zen, they sometimes talk about "*joriki*", which is a kind of concentrated inner power that develops from persistent *zazen*. Anyone can experience this within days, but I've never seen it to the degree of Shinzan. He is 80 but has the vigour, the life energy, of an infant. Not wild, like an infant, but completely grounded. He can be very still and frequently is, but there is no doubt of the potential force within him, just as you'd think of a tiger sat watching you. It comes across as a blazing presence which doesn't seem to get depleted no matter how he behaves.

Comparing him to an animal seems about right: intuitive, aligned, natural, and somehow impossible to get a hold on. Maybe it's those same qualities that are so attractive to be around; they stir a primal calling in us to be the same, to be liberated. Actually just comparing him to nature seems better. It's honestly like, on the one hand, he is an elderly Japanese gentleman, and on the other, he is an embodiment of something everybody knows well but didn't know was allowed to exist as a human being.

His dismissal of me from his room was the most compassionate thing he could have done. When I returned to my seat and sat down, all that headstrong energy had nowhere to go and fizzled out. Everything fell into a kind of openness, an innocence, and I'm pretty sure I shed a few tears of gratitude.

Ed with Shinzan Rōshi just after he took his precepts in July 2014

Alex Horikitsune Reinke

In May 2011 Shinzan Rōshi stayed with my family. It was a wonderful opportunity to get to know him more personally. Two little incidents stick in my mind. I remember him crossing the corridor to the bathroom one evening. He had no shirt on and, coming through a doorway, I was confronted by his aged body. How could this frailty develop such awesome power? I realised his love for us, his students and was moved to tears.

At the time my daughter was just one year old. It was enchanting to see her and Shinzan Rōshi connect. The Zen term "*nari kiru*" means to become one and this is exactly what he did. He literally became a one year-old too, and together they explored the fresh wonder of the present moment. I caught one of their encounters in a photograph.

Shinzan Rōshi with Alex, his wife Bao and daughter Alva

Johanna Barclay

We were very lucky to have a two hour session with our friend, Noriko, who gave us a crash course in 'survival Japanese' before the retreat last year (2014) at Gyokuruji temple. Meeting Shinzan for the first time, in the garden of the temple, I stumbled my way through some greetings I had rehearsed, and he very kindly smiled and chuckled at my attempts.

Later, as we sat on the *tatami* floor facing one another in the *sanzen* room, he was welcoming, generous with his teaching, and completely clear about Zen practice. Seeing him sitting framed by the open sliding doors, the valley sides rising up, covered in trees, bamboo, creepers, lush green foliage, is an image I will never forget. He looked completely at home, as much as the trees growing on the slopes. There was a sense of safety, an easy laugh. Then stern, completely focussed teaching.

The direction was simple, and often repeating the same message. Each time it opened up another angle; the same core—viewed from different sides. A connection to nature. "Now living, now surely going dying." "Teach children." "When cooking - cooking, cooking, only cooking, cut off idle thinking." These are a few of the phrases he spoke in English. There were more, all directed towards this, being in harmony with our true nature. Beyond the language of 'this and that', English and Japanese. Shinzan embodies his teaching; simply being a force of nature.

About Zenways

Zenways (Zendo Kyodan) promotes and encourages activities and practices that enhance human wellbeing, balance and awakening (*satori* or *kenshō*—the enlightenment of Zen) in the modern world.